The Drovers' Roads of Wales II
Pembrokeshire and the South

The Drovers' Roads of Wales II
Pembrokeshire and the South

Text: Shirley Toulson
Photographs: Caroline Forbes

Whittet Books Ltd

(Title page)
In the Black Mountains — the drove across Talgarth Common.

First published 1992

Whittet Books Ltd, 18 Anley Road, London W14 0BY

Maps by Paul Minns

British Library Cataloguing in Publication Data

Toulson, Shirley
The drovers roads of Wales.
2 : Pembrokeshire and the South.
I. Title II. Forbes, Caroline
914.2904857

ISBN 0905483987 pbk

The author and publishers gratefully acknowledge the kind permission of the following to reproduce photographs on the pages listed: the Welsh Black Cattle Society (p. 14), Worsley Archive Collection (p. 11, p. 13 and p. 17)

Typeset by Phoenix Photosetting, Chatham, Kent
Printed and bound by The Bath Press

To the memory of Oliver Caldecott,
who inspired and published the first
Drovers' Roads of Wales

Contents

Acknowledgments

Wherever I went in the course of my researches for this book throughout Wales and its borders, I met with friendly and helpful interest. I would like to record my thanks in particular to the time that my fellow writers, Roscoe Howell, Pat Molloy and Dewi Davies, author of *The Brecknock Historian*, gave to talking to me and the patience with which they dealt with my questions. I am also greatly indebted to Joe Bryant and the staff of the Brecon Beacons National Park, who gave me desk space in their busy office, access to old maps, and who showed me some of the lost roads south of Brecon.

The library work was done in the National Library of Wales at Aberystwyth and the Institute of Agricultural History in Reading. I am most grateful for the help I received in both those places.

All the owners of the riding centres mentioned at the end of the chapters took time out of their extraordinarily busy schedules to tell me about their areas and to discuss bridleways. I must make particular mention of Sandra Cooke of the Longhouse Livery Stables, Priory Wood, who has researched the drovers' routes in her area most thoroughly, and who spent two days taking me along them.

My thanks also go to my friends, Richard Raynsford, Jane Whittle and Thérèse Surridge, who shared some of the best walks with me; and to Helena Jones of Trallong who re-awakened my delight in the story of the physicians of Myddfai.

Introduction

Fifteen years ago, I traced the routes through north and mid-Wales along which the Welsh black cattle were taken to the English grazing grounds and markets. Working on that book, *The Drovers' Roads of Wales*, took me through some wild and beautiful countryside, and led me into some obscure and fascinating crannies of social history. I was aware, however, that the title was somewhat of a misnomer, for I had not included south Wales in my study; and I am delighted that I have now been given the chance to look at the story of cattle movements in Pembrokeshire and the rest of Dyfed, Glamorgan and Gwent.

I shall be dealing mostly with the history of droving in the eighteenth and nineteenth centuries, but it is as well to remember that those drovers were following a tradition that was at least five or six hundred years old. Indeed it probably goes back long before that, for, like many ancient peoples, the Welsh counted their wealth by their cattle. So it is no coincidence that the one word *da* means 'cattle' as well as 'good'. The historian, Caroline Skeel, to whose work I was much indebted when I wrote the last book, recorded that 1312 was the first date she could discover for the purchase of Welsh cattle for royal and noble households. There is no doubt that unrecorded transactions were going on long before that, but in the fourteenth century the word *porthmon*, meaning 'drover', first appeared in Welsh literature. It is to Sir Hugh Rhys Rankin of Radnorshire, writing in the 1955 edition of *Agriculture*, that I owe the information about Henry V's order that as many cattle as possible be collected in Wales and driven to the cinque ports to supply his armies in France.

Sir Hugh reckoned that from 1600 as many as thirty thousand head of cattle were being driven from all over Wales to England each year. The richer country became so dependent on this supply that when a murrain ravaged the Welsh cattle in 1632, so that none could be driven across the border, they had to be supplanted by imports of Irish cattle. This proved to be a serious enough threat to the Welsh trade for all imports of Irish cattle to be prohibited at the end of the reign of Charles II.

In turning to look at this trade from south-west Wales, I have relied heavily on two contemporary writers: George Owen of Henllys (near Newport on the northern coast of the Pembrokeshire peninsula), who lived from 1557–1613; and Richard Fenton (1746–1821), who in 1796 edited Owen's *Description of Pembrokeshire*, first published in 1603. Sadly, Owen had little respect for the people of his country, and as a major landowner regretted the lack of enclosures which resulted in many young people having to be employed in herding, an occupation which he considered encouraged lazy and dissolute habits. 'I have by good account numbered three thousand young people to be brought up continually in herding of cattle within this shire,' he wrote, adding that they were 'put to this idle education when they first come to be ten or twelve years of age and turned to the open fields to follow their cattle'. He reckoned that these youngsters would continue in this occupation for ten or twelve years.

During that time, he said, their skin began to resemble smoked fish, for 'they are forced to endure the heat of the sun in his greatest extremity, to parch and burn their faces, hands, legs, feet and breasts in such sort as they seem to be more like tawny moors than people of this land, and then with the cold, frost, snow, hail, rain and wind they are so tormentedd having the skin on their legs, hands, face and feet all in chinkes and chappes (lyke chinkes of an elephant wherwith he is wont to take the flies that come thither to suck his blood) that poor souls they may well hold the opinion with the papists that there is a purgatory.'

The drovers, whose long-distance routes we shall be following, were mostly better off than those lads, who were employed to walk sheep, cattle and sometimes pigs and geese from the farms to the local markets and fairs. On the long droves to the east, four or five men on horseback accompanied each herd of cattle. Often the owners also made the journey, bowling along in a pony-trap and going ahead to make reservations at the inns and arrange grazing for the animals. Rich men like that, as well as the licensed drovers and casual labourers, were all called *porthmon*.

Although they had a reputation for roguery, the drovers on the whole were upright, responsible men. They had to be licensed to practise their trade, and in order to obtain a licence at quarter sessions they had to be over thirty and have a stake in the community as householders. The Welshmen, however, naturally kept to their own tongue, and it was this that disconcerted English farmers like John Smith, who flourished on the Surrey/Hampshire borders in the first half of the nineteenth

1890. Haverfordwest cattle fair on St Thomas's Green beneath Merlin's Hill.

century. His nephew, the Farnham wheelwright and author George Bourne (who also wrote under the name of Sturt) recalled that his uncle found the Welsh drovers who came to the Blackwater Fair to be 'upright men but close-fisted'. What really annoyed him, however, was when a group of them came to bargain with him 'talking in English as good as his own, and then suddenly turning to one another to gabble in a tongue he couldn't understand. He felt at a disadvantage then.'

Because of the nature of the law, it is reports of dishonest dealings rather than accounts of fair trading that tend to survive. One such report dating from 1623 and unearthed by J. H. Bettey (*Somerset and Dorset Notes and Queries*, vol. 3, 1986) also has the advantage of telling us something about the general method of cattle sales. This report relates to a case brought against John Williams of Castletown in Glamorgan by three Taunton men, who stated that in the previous year, Williams, 'a very greate and common buyer and seller of cattle', had made fourteen or fifteen journeys for this purpose across the British channel. They reported that 'he doth seldome or never retourne out of Wales into Somersetshire without bringing with him twenty beasts and most tymes many more, being some oxen, some heyfers and some steers'. He rarely kept cattle for more than a week, but 'as soone as he bought them at any fayre in Wales he brought them over into Someresetshire and there presently sould them'.

I should here make a distinction between fairs and markets. The latter were held on a regular weekly basis; and it was not usual for livestock to be offered for sale there. Cattle were mainly sold at the great three-day fairs held between June and November. The Haverfordwest fair took place around July 20th, in a town whose market according to George Owen specialized in 'beef, mutton, bacon, veal, goose, capon, kid, lamb, rabbits, turkey and all sorts of wildfowl', salted, cured and prepared for the farm kitchens. Although this was the greatest market, George Owen suggested that it was wiser to go to Tenby; and as for the markets at St David's and his home town of Newport they were 'not worth the speaking of, partly for that they be so small and bad; but especially for the abuse, for that the same is used every Sunday before service, even about sun rising'.

People would travel up to a hundred miles to sell and buy in these fairs and markets, according to Alan Everett's contribution to Volume IV of the *Agrarian History of England and Wales* edited by Joan Thirsk; and at many of the fairs the total cattle sales could run into several thousand animals. Many of the walks in this book will follow the routes along which the herds were driven from the scattered farms to be sold to the drovers at the fairs. And we shall frequently be walking from one market town to another for, as Alan Everett explains, the cattle were often driven 'from one fair or farm to another, and sold two or three times *en route*'.

In south Pembrokeshire this means that our walks run towards Narberth, Whitland and St Clears. We will avoid for good historical reasons the industrial area of Milford Haven. Charles Hassall, who, in 1794, wrote the *General View of the Agriculture of the County of Pembroke* for the newly formed Board of Agriculture, was annoyed that fat cattle could not be exported from the home port. He complained that it was absolute folly, and gave an example of an incident in which not a single ship of war was able to be supplied locally (presumably because of Admiralty restrictions). Pembrokeshire farmers, he wrote, 'having no market for fat oxen have to sell them lean to drovers'.

The drover-dealers in their turn had the problem of paying large sums for the cattle at the fairs, and then being unable to get any return on their money until they reached the English graziers. To help with that difficulty various lending banks were established. One of the most notable was Wilkins and Co., which started business in Brecon in 1778. By 1840, this company had extended its business throughout most of south Wales. David W. Howell, who included the history of agricultural banking in his *Land and People in Nineteenth Century Wales* (Routledge and Kegan Paul, London, 1976), recorded that this firm would advance

1890. Cattle fair in front of the cottages on St Thomas's Green, Haverfordwest.

sums of up to two thousand pounds for two or three months on the joint note of a drover and his surety. Walter Jones & Co. of Carmarthen were more generous. They required no surety and would advance up to eight thousand. Presumably their interest rates reflected their way of doing business; there can be no doubt that the bankers were often as likely to be rogues as the drovers; although it is usually the latter whose misdemeanours are recorded. William Jones was one such. We know him for his failure in 1792 to re-pay David Lewis, who had advanced him five hundred pounds to buy cattle at the fair in Newcastle Emlyn.

The bulk of the cattle being taken to the English grazing grounds from Cardiganshire, Carmarthenshire and west Brecon were hardy, black runts; but the favoured beasts, who represented the biggest capital outlay, came from Pembrokeshire and Glamorgan. Walter Davies, who published his *General View of the Agriculture of South Wales* in 1815, had good things to say about the 'brownish black or dark brown' sleek-coated animals of Glamorgan. In his view they were 'the most tractable breed known'. However, he claimed that the coal-black Pembrokeshire bullocks throve 'better than the Glamorgan on coarse fodder whether green or dry'. That must have been a great consideration for any drover picking out a herd for the long journey to the east, an opinion substantiated by Charles Hassall's claim that, 'All the English as well as the Welch drovers, who drive cattle out of this country to the feeding centres in England agree that the True Pembrokeshire ox is the favourite beast with the graziers.' When he wrote that in 1794 five-year-old Pembrokeshire steers were selling for ten guineas each. By 1814 the price had doubled', an increase due in part to the rising costs occasioned by the Napoleonic wars.

Sir Hugh Rhys Rankin reckoned that the small black runts weighed about four to five hundredweight at the time of their sale at the fairs, but would actually improve in weight during their 200-240 mile journey from Wales into England. Charles Hassall made the same claim for the Pembrokeshires. 'The Black Ox bears his journey well', he wrote,' and will improve in his flesh as much in 3 months as some will in five. The average weight of our oxen at five years old be taken at about fifty to fifty six stone. When in full beef some will run to eighty stone.'

The value of the cattle as draught oxen before they were sold to the drovers can best be assessed by George Owen's observation that at Caldey Island the ploughing was done with horses because the farmers 'dare not keep oxen for fear of pirates'. So as valuable working animals these oxen were often sent into England for that purpose. The Somerset historian, J. H. Bettey (see page 11), has unearthed records of fairs held at Whitedown on the Dorset/Somerset borders between 1637-1649. He found confirmation that many cattle were brought to these fairs from Llantwit Major in south Glamorgan to be sold as draught oxen.

Welsh Black cattle today.

Cattle were also brought into England for dairy purposes. In 1798, when William Marshall, an English landowner, prepared his report on the *Rural Economy of the Southern Counties*, he referred to the Welsh cattle that stocked the farms around Maidstone in Kent. 'The heiffers, which are brought in for milk, are mostly of the Pembrokeshire mould,' he noted and added that, 'Many of them make handsome cows, which are said to milk well, and to fat quickly. Several thousands, of different descriptions, are annually brought into the county. In the month of October the roads are everywhere full of them.'

The most sought-after of all the Pembrokeshire cattle came from the area around Castlemartin, and were said to be descendants of the prehistoric wild white aurochs. Although Walter Davies claimed that these 'white-faced Pembrokeshire beasts' were not favoured by the drovers, there are records of dealers coming to the Pembrokeshire fairs from all over Wales specifically to purchase the Castlemartin cattle.

The members of the Pembrokeshire Naturalist Field Club who came to Tenby on February 3rd, 1880, to hear Edward Laws talk about the origins of this famous, now lost, breed, were reminded of 'the occasional white beast with ears, nose and feet black' that could then be seen grazing among the herds of black cattle. Mr Laws propounded his thesis that these cattle were descendants of the old breed of the county, who came from the *Bos primogenus*, whose bones had been found in the caves of Caldey Island and near Laugharne. He distinguished these cattle, which he believed were introduced into Pembrokeshire by the Danes, with 'the little long-faced cattle of eastern origin which followed their neolithic and British masters into exile, driven from the fat pastures of England to the barren hills of Wales, and destined to perpetuate their dwarfed proportions in the breed known as Welsh runts.'

His thesis is possibly questionable, but one thing is certain: long before the drovers of the eighteenth and nineteenth centuries started to bid high for Castlemartin cattle, the white cattle from whom Edward Law claimed they were descended were highly prized throughout Wales. In the tenth century, Hywel Dda, Welsh king and law-giver, reckoned that a hundred white cows with red ears were worth a hundred and fifty black animals.

By 1874, when R. H. Harvey wrote his introductory article to the first volume of the Welsh Black Cattle Herd Book, the white animals described by Mr Laws had become exceedingly rare. Although he agreed that the few remaining were descended from *Bos primogenus* and related to the wild white cattle of Chillingham in Northumbria, he was more interested in their descendants. He claimed that 'Those who have seen a good Black Ox well fed have always acknowledged that there cannot be a handsomer animal.'

In his opinion the Pembrokeshire cattle owed their robust constitution to the fact that, 'The annual rainfall of the district occupied by the Black Cattle is about twice the amount of that of Chiswick; and the westerly winds are very strong. It therefore requires a hardy race to stand the exposure during the winter...This quality of hardiness is possessed by the Blacks; and they also in their coats and general appearance shew the first approach of the genial spring. There is no animal which commands so good a price in the fairs as a bullock that has been wintered out in the fields and shows fair condition and a good coat.'

Although the Pembrokeshire winters may be wet, they are relatively free of snow, a situation which boded well for sheep also, who in George Owen's estimation did not need winter feeding. He tells us that the flocks were gathered together for shearing in May, the wool being either sent directly to markets in Bristol, Barnstaple and Somerset or sold directly to English buyers, who came regularly into south-west Wales for the best bargains.

The sheep as well as their wool were taken into England, in separate droves from the cattle. Some of them were driven to the ports of south Wales and taken by boat across the Bristol Channel for sale in Minehead, Chard or Taunton. Others were driven into the English Midlands and southern counties, many of the flocks going right across the country to be sold at Harrow-on-the-Hill, a trade that lasted eighty years, from 1820 to 1900. John Smith reported that Welsh sheep came into his part of the country in flocks numbering anything from fifteen hundred to two thousand. 'Wild as rabbits they were,' he told his nephew, 'but there were two or three dogs with the men, and the dogs did all the work.'

In the seventeenth century, George Owen recorded that there were 'also sold yearly great droves of whethers, young sheep and lambes, and those driven by land to be sold in England which also bringeth some money to the countrye; so is used hogs and swine which people do breed and spare more than serveth their own turns.' Walter Davies in his *General View of the Agriculture of South Wales* affirmed that the drovers were divided in their preferences for the 'old stock-eared' breed of hog, or 'the short-eared Chinese'. Different markets would specialize in one or other of these types, depending on which drovers were likely to attend them.

Whatever breed was chosen, the drovers, some of whom were Englishmen heading directly for the Bristol markets, had a long and tedious journey ahead of them. For pigs will only travel about six miles a day, and that reluctantly, whereas a herd of cattle could be expected to cover twenty.

1915. Landgirls driving cattle to the fair at Haverfordwest.

During the first half of the nineteenth century, a hired drover could expect to receive ten shillings a week plus expenses from the dealer, who could expect to make substantial sums of money on his transactions; but who also took the risk of loss through cattle murrain or changes in market prices. Each drover would be responsible for about a hundred bullocks. He was usually mounted and would have a corgi dog acting as heeler to keep the herd together. A drove could well be made up of four or five hundred head of cattle, and in many cases the dealer employing the drovers would ride or drive behind the herds and settle up at the inns for the men's food and shelter and the beasts' pasture.

It was also vital that the animals be watered on the route, and you will find that many drovers' roads go past specially constructed or reinforced natural ponds. The drovers had to be sure of their location and be able to make an accurate calculation as to the time it would take the animals to reach them. This need for constant water was especially important for the dark-brown cattle of Glamorgan, a breed particularly favoured for being easy to handle and for the very fine quality of the beef. Walter Davies quotes an English drover he met at the Newcastle Emlyn fair, who told him that the Glamorgans are liable to 'fall off more in long summer journeys, through dry countries'.

As I noted in my previous book, inns offering accommodation to drovers usually advertised their presence by planting one or two Scots pines on an otherwise barren hillside. This holds true also in south Wales, and we shall come across the sites of many such erstwhile inns marked in this way.

I also explained in my previous book how the cattle were shod for their long journey to the east; and the sites of smithies, many on the sites of forges operating for the shoeing of horses until farm work became mechanized, is also an indication of the routes that were taken. Only a very few are marked on the maps, but people who now live in them are usually proud to display 'The Old Forge' as the name of their house. Sometimes the shoeing was done on the journey by a smith with a portable forge; and even more frequently a beast might be shod cold in a makeshift way by one of the drovers. Spare shoes were always carried along on the journey together with a supply of short nails. The latter were always wrapped in a piece of bacon fat so that they should not go rusty and cause gangrene if the animal's flesh should be pierced inadvertently. Sir Hugh Rhys Rankin wrote that in the late nineteenth century the shoeing charge was a shilling a beast; and he explained that the *cws*, or cattle shoes, were sometimes made out of disused pony shoes, cut in half and nailed on either side of the cloven hoof. In his opinion there were two essentials for choosing the routes along which the shod cattle might be driven: the way must provide plenty of good grazing and fresh water; and it must be at least fairly dry underfoot. So marshes and flooded areas were avoided, and the route taken was always the driest rather than the shortest.

A day's journey lasted anything from twelve to fourteen hours, the cattle never going faster than two miles an hour, the pace which I also reckon on when I am walking over rough ground. Often you will come across lanes with exceptionally wide verges along which cattle could graze, and this is usually an indication of a much-used drove route; as Sir Hugh pointed out, 'Before enclosures, the beasts could spread out on the hillside' and graze there.

Until the turnpike trusts with their heavy toll charges were set up, cattle were driven directly to the destinations along such roads as existed. Walter Davies claimed that in the mid-sixteenth century, roads were of two kinds: they were either deep in the centre of the plain or valley, or they ran 'steep up the brow of a hill'. The first he considered public ditches, the second public step ladders.

By the end of the eighteenth century, the turnpike trusts were formed to improve the roads. Charles Hassall advised the builders to repair the surfaces 'more generally with field stones' and so save the expense of taking stone from quarries. He added that further savings might be made if the gathering of these stones was done 'by women and children at so much a load'. With such an attitude rife among the gentry responsible for the turnpikes, it is no wonder that there was general dissatisfaction and unrest among the population at large as the new roads came into being and increasingly heavy tolls were imposed on anyone taking beasts to fairs and markets. In the late 1830s this unrest flared up into the Rebecca Riots, a movement which was to become allied with the Chartist demonstrations in south Wales. These oddly named riots had their beginnings in Pembrokeshire, and they are explained more fully when we visit Efailwen in the course of the first chapter. It was at the toll gate there that Rebecca's wrath first publicly exploded.

The turnpike roads have now mostly become our trunk roads; and although the tolls were an unmitigated curse to the drovers, they prove a hidden blessing to any walker following the routes taken by the herds. For naturally the drover dealers would do anything to avoid paying the charges, even if it meant taking devious routes across wild country. 'They'd lose a day goin' round, sooner'n they'd pass a gate,' John Smith told his nephew. So following them is more interesting and pleasant for us. As far as I can, I have indicated where the routes I have followed were taken in order to avoid paying toll dues.

It was the coming of the railways that eventually put a stop to droving; although until the advent of motor transport cattle, sheep and pigs still had to be walked to the railhead. In south Wales most of the livestock were taken to Cowbridge in mid-Glamorgan. By that time many of the animals were not destined for the English markets but as provisions for the growing colliery towns of the Rhondda and Ebbw Vale. David W. Howell has estimated that when the railways took over from the drovers thirteen thousand head of cattle left Carmarthenshire annually, 10,000 came out of Pembrokeshire and 7,000 from Cardiganshire.

Of recent years a sort of romanticism, to which I confess I may have contributed, has attached itself to the drovers and their long journeys taking cattle across wild country. Although I do not agree with those writers who say that droving was essentially a coarse and cruel matter, I have to acknowledge that most of the animals were destined for slaughter, a matter that most of us meat-eaters do not like to dwell on.

Nevertheless, as the question of animal transportation becomes more and more urgent for our own times, and as we are continually being shocked and distressed by stories of desperately callous cruelty to the cattle and sheep destined for continental abattoirs, it is one that we must face. Those farmers who today talk of 'growing sheep' as though they were cabbages are unlikely to be familiar with W. H. Davies's haunting poem 'Sheep' about sailing with a flock of 1,800 from Baltimore to Glasgow.

The first night we were out at sea
  Those sheep were quiet in their mind;
The second night they cried with fear –
  They smelt no pastures in the wind.

They sniffed, poor things, for their green fields,
  They cried so loud I could not sleep:
For fifty thousand shillings down
  I would not sail again with sheep.

I am pretty sure that Welsh poet was a meat-eater, and so was the Devonian novelist and playright, John Galsworthy. Yet that sensitive, fastidious and compassionate man forced himself to visit abattoirs, and successfully campaigned for many reforms as a result of what he saw.

Mass, mechanized agriculture has taken us a long way from those comparatively caring and careful pre-war days; yet I do not believe that the people actually in charge of the animals are indifferent to the cruelty of the conditions they are forced to impose. Losing my way on a winter walk in Wiltshire recently, I accepted a lift back to base from an elderly man driving a van, which turned out to be taking three large cows to slaughter. This kindly man was truly distressed that the animals were packed in so small a space. 'They are too many, they are too big,' he said with real sadness in his voice.

I am sure that many of the eighteenth- and nineteenth-century drovers whose course we shall be following had similar feelings; quite apart from the fact that if they wanted to deliver the animals to the graziers in good condition, they had to see that they were well treated on the way. They were not all entirely motivated by profit. Even the hard-headed Charles Hassall, who thought nothing of commending the cheap labour of women and children, was concerned to see oxen, eventually destined for the English graziers, working in the fields as draught animals. 'It is painful', he wrote, 'to see oxen driven beyond what their strength can bear, and in a manner the wise Author of nature never designed for them.'

His sentiments are in tune with a thirteenth-century commendation that, 'The priest ought to inquire of the penitent if he was accustomed to curse men or other creatures; for to be vehemently angry with God's creatures or with cattle, and to curse them, even with the ill-will to harm them, which countrymen often do, cursing men and innocent animals, is a great sin.' I believe that the feeling that inspired Thomas Chabham, sub-dean of Salisbury, when he penned that section of his *Summa de Pentitentia* is still alive, and that it was shared by many of the Welsh and English drovers whose livelihood depended on the cattle trade.

The Drovers' Routes - A User's Guide

The walks in this book, some of which are linear, some circular, are divided according to area by chapter; in one or two cases, such as that of the route of the Sarn Helen from Neath to Brecon, you will find that the walk runs across two chapters. Even in that instance, however, it might well be more convenient to make the walk in two stages, and you will find that the approximate length of each section is given on the appropriate map, as it is for all the other walks in this book.

Paul Minns's maps are designed to orientate the reader and to present an overall picture of the areas covered by each chapter. They are not intended to be accurate walking guides. For those you must turn to the Ordnance Survey Landranger, or even better the 2½ inch Pathfinder series. To help you locate your position on those official maps, you will find grid references in brackets: the first number is the OS map number and it is followed by the grid reference. The walks have been given letters of the alphabet, which are also located on the maps.

I allow a pace of about two miles an hour for walking in rough country, which is about the same speed at which cattle and sheep were driven. Pigs, who cannot be prevented from rooting on the way, no matter how much they are muzzled, go a lot slower. You will probably go somewhat faster on level ground, but it is best to allow some extra time to investigate places along the way. So the two miles an hour estimate is a wise calculation. A few of the walks will take you across trackless areas of high moorland, and in some places in the hills it is not always easy to differentiate between the main path and sheep-runs. This does not present much of a problem in clear weather when it is easy enough to focus on landmarks, but when sudden clouds or mists come down you may find yourself relying on a compass, so it is essential to take one with you. In these more remote areas it is also a good idea to take an ordinary sports whistle; *six blasts* is the emergency signal, and, if you should get into trouble, it will make it easier for a rescue service to find you. For the same reason, if you are making one of the longer walks in an isolated area, do let somebody know of your plans, and the approximate time at which they can expect to hear from you.

At the end of most chapters you will find suggested riding centres for the area. It would be wise to check with them if you want to follow any of the drove routes on horseback, for some authentic bridleways are so overgrown that they are almost impassable in summer, and others may be under dispute with the landowners.

Because this book is so much concerned with the routes along which cattle were driven from the farms to the local fairs, and then from one fair to another before making the long trek to the east for the English markets, or south to the channel crossings, it makes no claim to be exhaustive. Many readers will want to set out on their own investigations and there are one or two guidelines to help you in your searches. They are all mentioned in the course of describing the routes in this book, but a checklist could be helpful, so I suggest that you bear the following points in mind:

1. Toll routes, toll bridges, toll houses and toll gates

It is usually fairly easy to locate the situations where tolls were collected. The wayside toll house set at an angle to the road with its windows facing in all directions is particularly easy to detect. Remember that the drovers would endure long detours and some difficult hill country rather than pay exorbitant tolls. So if you find a lane or track roughly parallel to the main road, you can be sure that cattle were once taken along it. Toll bridges are another matter. You may still have to use them as a way of crossing a river, but if you can locate the position of former fords that the drovers would certainly have used, you can start to work out the tracks leading to them on both sides of the water. Lanes with particularly wide verges are usually an indication that droves of cattle were taken along them and were able to graze on the way; and on open country the old tracks are still often lined by the remnants of earthbanks planted with hawthorn.

2. Shoeing stations

These are less easy to locate, but we know that there were shoeing stations near all the great cattle fairs; there the cattle were shod for the first stages of their journey to the east. I have noted the main ones such as that to the north of the market town of Narberth. One shoeing, however, was never sufficient for the whole route and so there are many other minor shoeing stations to be found on the way. They are not always easy to find. Here, as I have indicated, you can exercise a little detective skill by noticing houses still carrying the name of the old forge, and by remembering that many remote garages and petrol stations are sited on former smithies.

3. Inns

The drovers needed rest and refreshment along the way for themselves as well as overnight grazing for their cattle. Hostelries and inns that offered such facilities frequently advertised themselves by planting Scots pines beside the building, setting them in such a way that they could be visible for many miles. There is still an inn actually called The Scotch Pine, just outside Ammanford (see Chapter 6). There is no pine tree there now — the reverse of the usual situation, for you are much more likely to find pines but no inn. In such cases, further investigations around such lone trees will probably reveal the ruins of former buildings or those of a nearby farmhouse.

4. Farms

Many remote hill farms once brewed their own beer, and may also have served as inns, so we must get away from our image of the public house with its bars, when we are looking for drovers' inns. Whether the farms served as inns or not, the walks in this book will take you past the sites of many ancient farmsteads, for I have been particularly concerned with the routes from individual farms, where some of the drovers made direct deals, to the cattle fairs which could be twenty miles away or more.

Reservoir waters and dense rows of conifers have drowned many of the farms and the direct routes from them to the fairs; so some of the walks I describe have had to be based on conjecture. Except for parts of Brechfa Forest (Chapter 6), I have tended to avoid long walks through the trees, as I find they can be dark and monotonous. I must warn you, however, that in some cases you will find yourself walking through trees where none are shown on even a fairly recent Ordnance Survey map, although they are indicated on the maps that illustrate this book. Commercial conifers run to a thirty-year crop cycle on average, and unless you subscribe to the expensive Ordnance Survey up-dating service, you will find that the cartographers simply have not kept up with the pace of felling and re-planting.

Finally, do remember to take some emergency food and drink with you on these walks, for there is not much possibility of finding anything on the way; if you should get lost or stranded, raisins, chocolate and oranges (which are not too heavy to carry) can be life-savers. For the same reason it is wise to take a supply of warm clothing (there is a lot to be said for woolly hats as a way of retaining body heat) and always wear strong boots. I also find that a stick is useful for testing boggy ground. Some of the country you will be crossing is more isolated now than it was when the drovers took the great herds of black cattle to the east, and, however friendly and hospitable the hills appear, they must always be treated with respect.

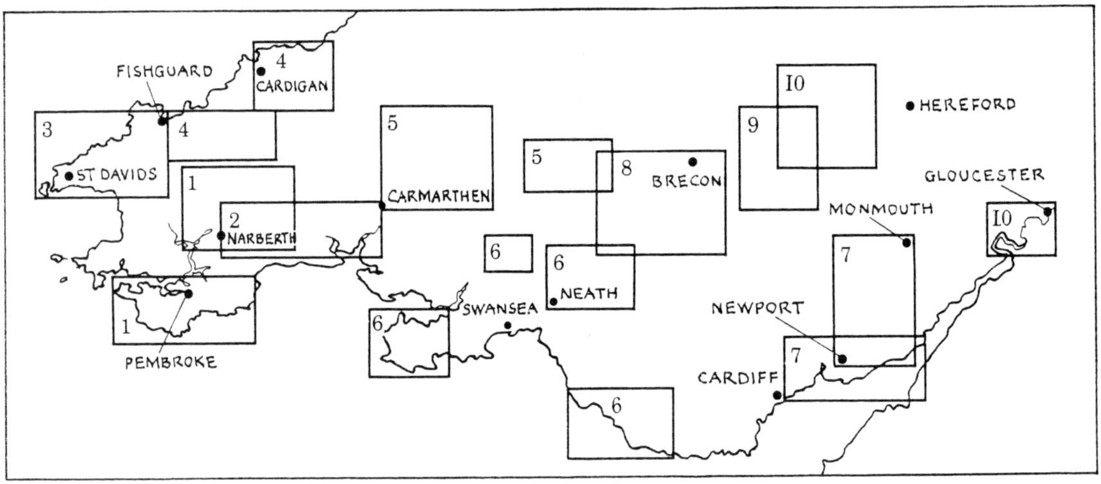

Chapter 1

The Englishry: to Narberth and Whitland

From the lush meadows of the Angle peninsula and the farms of south Pembrokeshire, the drovers started on their journeys to the grazing grounds of eastern England. Some would be two months on the way. The cattle came from the rich, loamy country south of the Landsker, the line of Norman castles stretching from east to west, built to protect these southern, fertile lands, which the conquerors kept for their own cultivation. The Welsh were left with the wilder, upland terrain to the north.

The hundred of Castlemartin, which extended eastwards to the vale of St Florence running inland from Tenby, was particularly rich; Charles Hassall of Narberth, who wrote *The General View of the Agriculture of the County of Pembroke* in 1794 for the newly formed Board of Agriculture, described its soil as 'being equally grateful to the grazier and the plowman'.

This is the area that gave its name to the most esteemed strain of Welsh black cattle, as Clare Sewell Read confirmed in 1849, when he wrote in the journal of the Royal Agricultural Society that, 'The best Pembrokeshire cattle are bred in the district of Castlemartin and they are principally called by the name of that hundred' (see also Introduction, page 15).

Cattle were not the only beasts to be driven east out of Pembrokeshire. Writing in 1603, George Owen of Henllys in the north of the county declared that, 'There are also sold yearly great droves of whethers, young sheep and lambs, and those driven by land to be sold in England which also bringeth some money to the countrye; so is used hogs and swine which the people do breed and spare more than serveth their own turns.' Two hundred years later, Walter Davies in the *General View of the Agriculture of South Wales* noted that the Pembrokeshire store pigs were called by the Flemish name of 'iggies'. These pigs were driven east to be sold in Bristol, a long, tedious journey as anyone who has ever been responsible for moving pigs from one field to the next will affirm.

A Angle → Bosherston 13 miles
B Bosherston → Merlin's Cross 12 miles
C Tenby → Sageston 6 miles

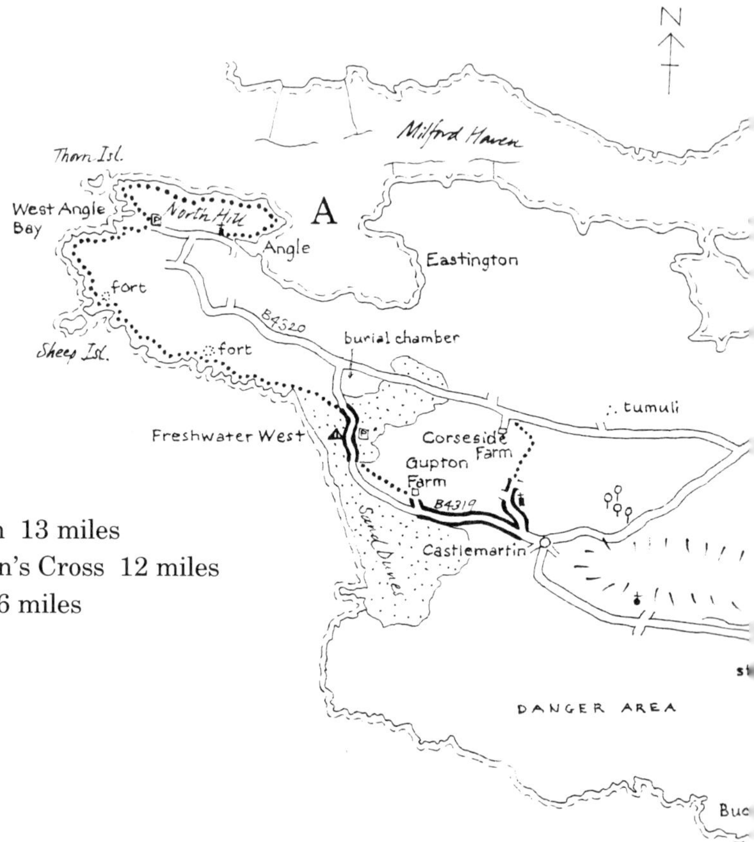

A Unfortunately the land to the south of Castlemartin village is now owned by the Ministry of Defence, and is only accessible by special arrangement. However it is possible to explore some of the coastal fields where these famous cattle were reared. I shall start off from Angle itself, the little harbour on the west side of Angle Bay, for the eighteenth-century farm buildings at Eastington, on the other side of the water, are almost obscured by one of the oil refineries of Milford Haven. In any case, Angle (157:865029) is worth giving a little time to on its own account. There is a strange remnant of a castle here, consisting of a single fortified tower of the sort that one usually expects to find in Ireland or the Scottish borders. There is a dovecote close by, and around it there are signs of the strip fields, marked out when this was a feudal village.

From Angle you can take the lane directly past the church to West

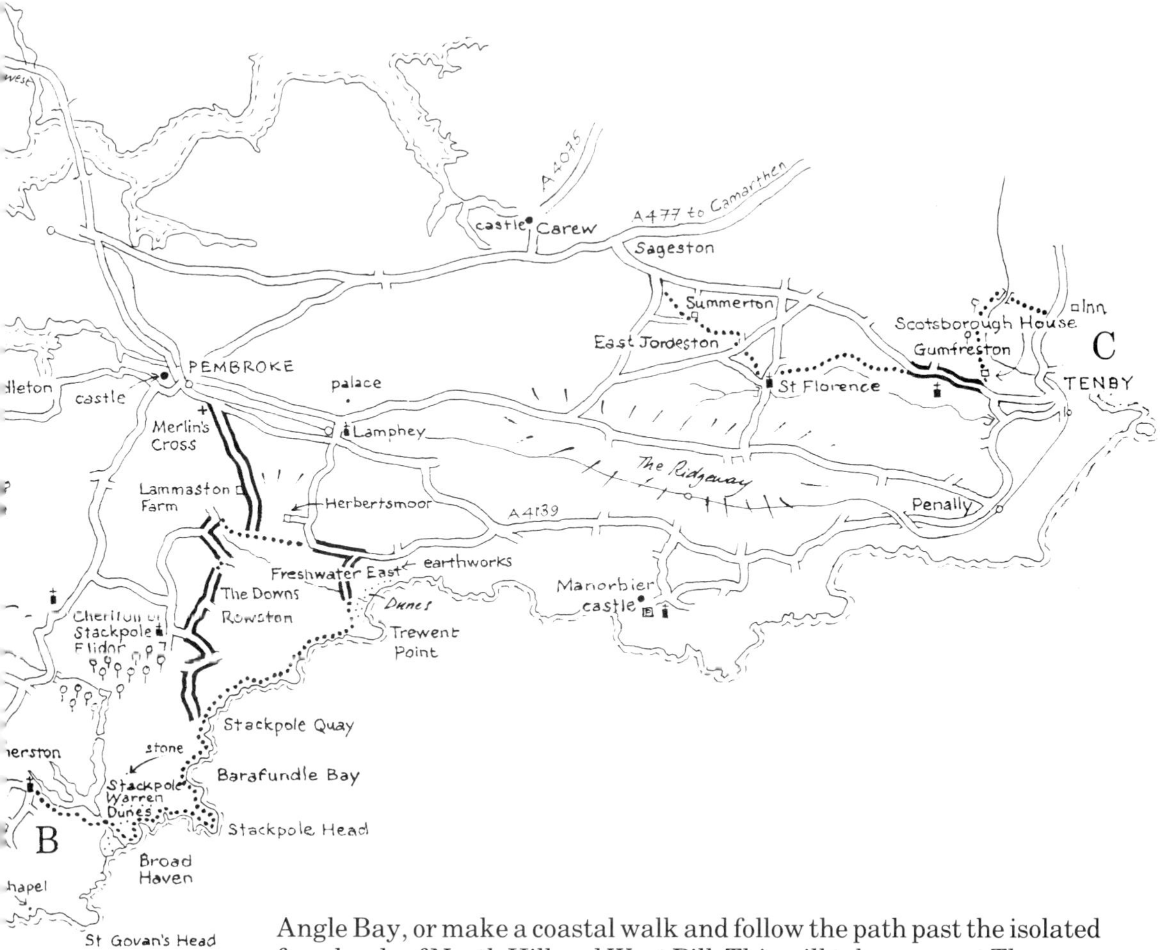

Angle Bay, or make a coastal walk and follow the path past the isolated farmlands of North Hill and West Pill. This will take you past Thorn Island, known for years as Rat Island (like the rock across the bay) and described by George Owen as being 'Verie litle, full of deep grasse'. Now it is saddled with a formidable rectangular building, once used for military purposes and currently serving as an hotel. If you take this path, you will reach the bay by the ruins of a limekiln, where stone brought here by sea was prepared for the further enrichment of the fields. It seems an inhospitable landing place, the beach being narrowly enclosed by ridges of jagged, sea-furrowed grey rock.

To the south the coastal path runs for four miles on the top of forbidding cliffs. It passes the ruins of Tudor defences opposite the smaller Rat Island, and the earthworks of an Iron Age camp on Sheep Island.

There is another Celtic fortification between West and East Pickard Bays.

The coastal path joins the B4319 three miles out of Castlemartin, but you can continue a coastal walk across the sand dunes of Freshwater West. It is most unsafe and unwise to even consider bathing from here because of quicksands and treacherous currents; but it is worth walking a little way across the shifting sands for the sake of a most unusual building: a seaweed gatherer's hut, used for drying the wide, curled, salty ribbons that were made into laver bread. An information panel describing that process can be found inside the hut: a precarious, ramshackle lean-to, roofed by three rows of ragged thatch reaching down to the ground.

A track goes inland from here by Gupton Farm (158:894990), and then you must follow the B4319 to Castlemartin itself, on the edge of the artillery ranges. It is a tiny village now, mainly notable for the eighteenth-century, ruined, stone cattle pound, which has been incorporated into the roundabout on the main road to the east of the village.

During the seventeenth century, the tracks in this area were frequented by itinerant Irish, riding on horseback and carrying whiskey from farm to farm. They had swarmed in because of the Irish wars, and George Owen wrote that they were 'so powdered among the inhabitants of Castlemartin, that in every village you shall find the third, fourth or fifth householder an Irishman'. They occupied themselves 'in the making of aquavite (whiskey) in great abundance' and then carried it around the neighbourhood 'so that weekly you may be sure to have aquavite to be sold at your door'.

If you go north from Castlemartin, past the battlemented tower of the church, you can walk over the drained fen of Castlemartin Corse and climb up to the B4320 by Corseside Farm. Mr Campbell of Stackpole Court drained the fen in the 1790s, a work for which he was publicly commended by Charles Hassall, who commented that he had transformed 'a perfect bog' and declaring, 'No agricultural improvement that I have been a witness of in the course of extensive and long experience, has succeeded better than this undertaking.' Nevertheless, despite Hassall's praise for the most wealthy of his neighbours, the 'corse' was still being described as a 'peaty morass' in 1849, and so no cattle would have been brought this way. They would have had to follow the lane over Axton Hill (158:933988), through Hundleton to Pembroke; which can be quite busy with traffic in summer now. So I should like to end this short walk at Corseside and turn to look at some of the routes taken from the southern farms around Bosherston on the south-eastern edge of the ranges.

St Govan's chapel in a cleft of the rocks of the south Pembrokeshire coast.

Bridge across Bosherston lily ponds.

B

Bosherston is a pretty village attracting hordes of summer visitors, who come to see the famous chapel in the cleft of the rocks to the west of St Govan's Head, and, especially in early summer, to delight in the eighty acres of water lilies covering three narrow, artificial lakes beneath the Norman church. You can walk beside them down to the sands at Broad Haven and from there take the path across the dunes of Stackpole Warren. All this land belonged to the worthy Mr Campbell.

It was in 1688 that the vast Stackpole estate first came into his family's hands, when Alexander Campbell of Cawdor took possession of it. We shall walk over more of his territory in the east, when we come to explore the rich pastures of Golden Grove beside the Teifi. In Pembrokeshire, the estate, besides stretching northwards to Castlemartin and Angle, extended from Freshwater West to Freshwater East.

If you follow the coastal path round Stackpole Head, you will come to

Huntsman's leap by St Govan's Head.

the dunes to the west of Barafundle Bay. Until myxomatosis struck the rabbits here in the 1950s, these warrens provided a healthy cash crop for the local people.

To continue north-east, over the springy, flower-bedecked turf of the wide down to Stackpole Quay, you must climb up from the sand to the wall built by the Cawdors in the late eighteenth century, at the same time that the Bosherston lakes were flooded and the tiny harbour was constructed to the north-east. Once limestone was shipped from Stackpole Quay to farms along the coast and to the limekilns of West Angle Bay; now the little harbour is used almost entirely by lobster fishermen, and for the collection of oysters from the off-shore beds.

The farms to the north of the harbour, one of which is almost on the cliff edge, sent their cattle to the Pembroke market through the village of Stackpole Elidor (158:988974). You can follow their route along the lane, turning east to the cluster of farms at Rowston. From there you can cross over the downs by a footpath, turn left to take a lane down into the valley; and when you have crossed a stream you will find a footpath on your right going along a hillside to Freshwater East. Follow it until you meet the track going north to Lammaston Farm.

If you prefer one more cliff-top walk, you can approach that point from Freshwater East itself; but do not attempt the stretch of the coastal path east from Stackpole Quay in wet or misty weather, for it is a steep and extremely narrow, slippery passage with the farmer's fence closing it in one side and the drop over the cruel Stackpole cliffs threatening it on the other. Long before this land was enclosed, Henry II went hawking along these cliff-tops, and he considered the falcons that were bred here were the best in the world. It is still a good place for watching sea-birds.

The wide, safe bathing beach of Freshwater East attracts many visitors, and the walker, who has to join the B4584 leading out of it, will do best not to cross the sands but to take the lane running past the camp sites to the west of the town. A walk of about a mile along this B road will bring you to the hillside footpath leading to the farm track to Lammaston. From there the way is clear, running just west of north to Merlin's Cross on the outskirts of Pembroke.

The cattle that had been collected at Pembroke were mostly sent north-east towards Narberth, following a route now largely covered by the A477, running through Sageston to the south of Carew castle. Along this route they would have been joined by the herds from the farms around Tenby, and those cattle which were towed behind barges or forced to swim from Caldey Island to the beach below Giltar Point, seaward from Penally (now serving as a Ministry of Defence rifle range). Ashore the cattle would have joined flocks of poultry and wildfowl being taken to Tenby market.

Entrance to the harbour of Stackpole Quay.

Lydstep Haven, across the water from Caldey Island.

The droves going inland from Tenby were covering the route traversed by the fisherwomen of Llangwym, above the Daugleddau estuary where the eastern and western Cleddau rivers run into the sea. These hardy women rowed downstream to Carew and then walked the remaining ten miles to Tenby. Their descendants were still making the journey to sell their wares in the holiday town in the 1960s, but by then they no longer did it on foot, nor did they wear the red woollen shifts, plaid scarfs and black 'bowler' hats that Frith found to be their traditional gear, when he painted one such fisherwoman selling oysters to his wife and daughters in 1880.

It is tempting to linger in the walled town of Tenby, and to make the gentle climb above the beach to the ruins of the thirteenth-century castle to watch the boats plying between Caldey Island and the mainland; and even, if you are here in March, to relish the long-trumpeted narcissi peculiar to the region and given the name of Tenby daffodils in 1796. To the drovers they must have been a signal: when their blooms were done it was time to prepare for the long summer journey. Some of them may also even have known the redoutable bathing machine attendant, Peggy Davis, who is remembered by a plaque in the parish church of St Mary recording that she served the town's female visitors 'with good humour and respectful attention' until she died in 1809 of an apoplectic fit in the water, while she was looking after the ladies in her care. She was then 82.

C There are two historic routes out of Tenby. One is the ancient track along the ridgeway that links the town to Pembroke. Its wide verges suggest that it was a main route for the cattle droves. The other route goes north-east more or less on the course of the B4318 through Gumfreston. I plan to look at the farmland lying between these two thoroughfares, but before setting out on that journey it is worth making a slight detour to the north in order to look at the ivy-clad ruins of Scotsborough House (158:118013). This was the home of the Ap Rees family in the seventeenth century. They also have a memorial in St Mary's church.

You reach the remains of their mansion, deserted since the early nineteenth century, by taking the main Tenby to Narberth road as far as the inn (158:128009) and then following Folly Lane under the railway bridge. Follow the woodland lane south from here past Folly Cottage to the ruins of the Scotsborough Lodge gates and the traces of the avenue that the family planted to enhance their estate. Their noble driveway is now reduced to an overgrown track beside a muddy lane which leads past the house to the B4318. Turn right here and you will soon see the beckoning, tapering tower of Gumfreston's thirteenth-century church.

Half a mile past the church and its three attendant holy wells by the churchyard, you will come to a path on your left running north-west above the Ritec marshes. Across the valley you can see the ridge stretching towards Pembroke and now marking the southern boundary of the National Park. The valley itself was once an inlet of the sea, making it possible to get right up to Scotsborough House by boat. The path you are on will bring you across a small tributary flowing into this valley to the centre of St Florence village. Some of the herds from the farms in this area must have gone directly north to the Narberth markets along the lanes running through Jeffreyston (158:090065), whence local farmers sent cattle to the fairs at Pembroke and Maenclochog, and so avoided the crushing tolls imposed by the turnpike trust on the main road running east from Haverfordwest. We shall look at some other routes that were taken in order to avoid these heavy charges in the next walk. Now let us take the path going north-west from St Florence by the farms of East Jordeston and Summerton to the B4318 and the road to Sageston.

Some of the cattle were brought east from the fair at Haverfordwest to Narberth and the first shoeing station at Caermaenau Fawr (158:120166), where a blacksmith fixed the *cws* or cues (two half-moons to protect each cloven hoof), the iron having previously been prepared at Bryn Hill to the south of Narberth. The wretched beasts would be thrown and shod many more times before they reached the temporary havens of the English grazing grounds.

Now I want to consider the problems facing those drovers who wanted to avoid the heavy charges imposed along those routes which began to be turnpiked from 1771 along the highway from Haverfordwest to the east. To follow some of the diversions they would have made we can make exploratory walks north and south of Arnolds Hill, four miles to the east of Haverfordwest along the A40.

Di The first walk takes us north across the valley of Millin Brook to South

Di Arnolds Hill → Wiston Castle 4 miles
Dii Arnolds Hill → Narberth 10 miles
E Maenclochog → A478 7 miles
F Efailwen → Whitland 16 miles

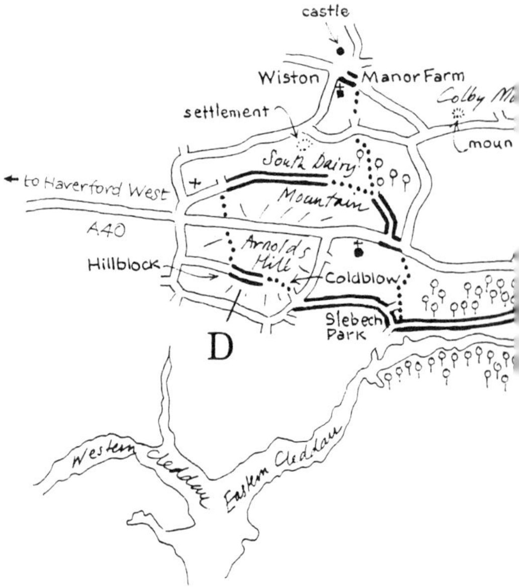

Dairy Mountain. Follow that ridgeway to the east and then go north through Wiston Wood, descending to the valley of the Fenton Brook. On the other side of that stream you can climb up to the Manor Farm by Wiston church, behind which you can make out the remaining stones of Wiston castle, standing on private ground. There are records that cattle

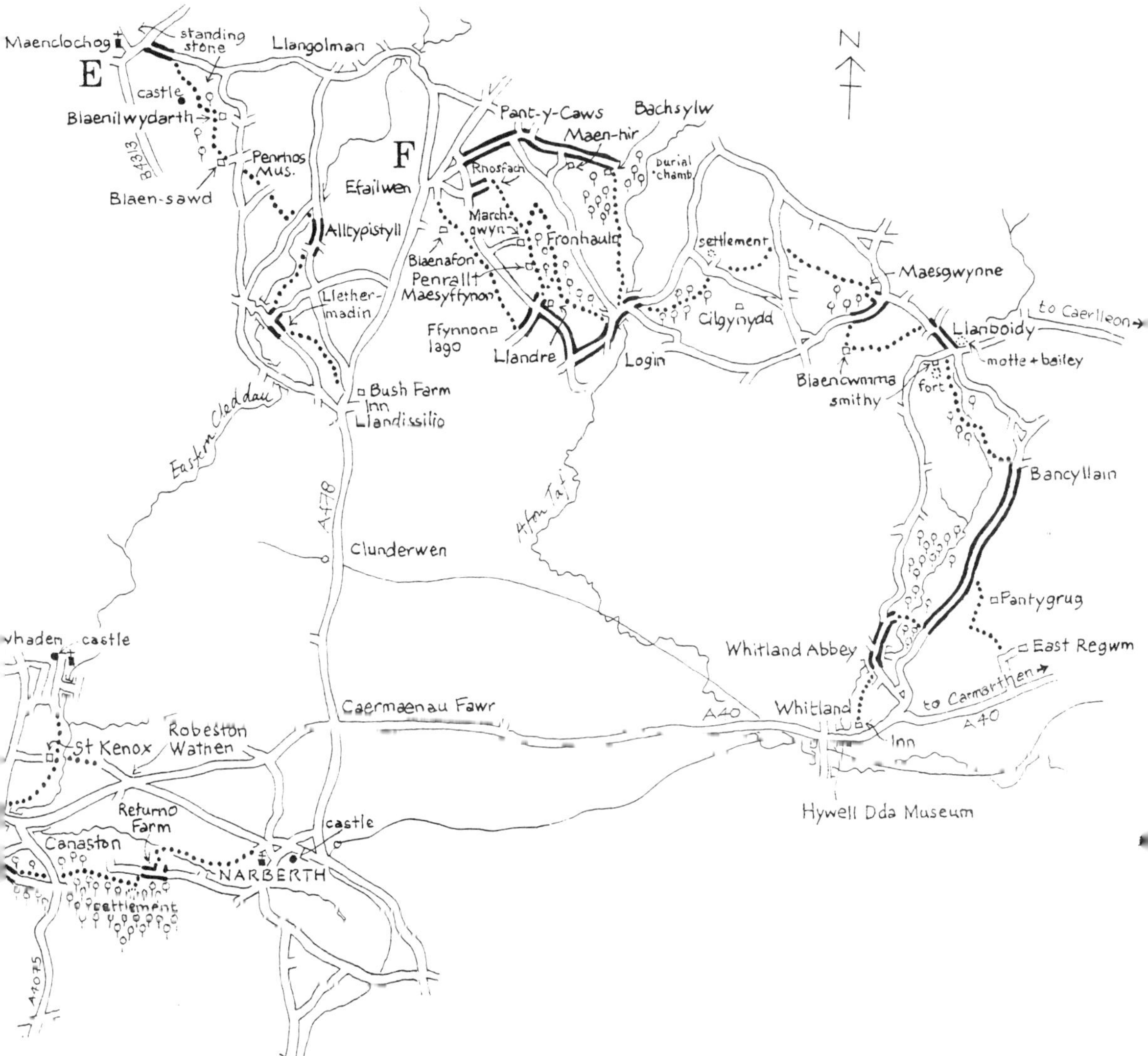

were brought to the fair at Wiston from 1690.

The castle was built by Wizo, a delightfully named but much resented Flemish settler, who came to south Wales at the beginning of the twelfth century when many families from the Netherlands, invited by the Norman landowners, were settling in Pembrokeshire. Henry I granted this Wizo extensive lands between the Western and Eastern Cleddau rivers, and his primitive motte and bailey constructed to defend these acres was later strengthened by his sons, only to be razed to the ground by Llewellyn's forces in 1220. It was restored in the reign of Edward I, by Sir John Wogan, the king's justiciary of Ireland, who married Gwenllian, heiress to Wiston, but of that building only the walls of the keep now remain.

A lane runs east from here to Llawhaden, where the next walk begins,

Ruins of Llawhaden Castle above the Eastern Cleddau.

and once again we are on the site of a battleground as we cross Colby Moor, the scene of a decisive victory for the Parliamentarians in the Civil War, when General Rowland Laugharne totally routed the Royalist forces on July 29th, 1645.

There was a toll gate at Plain Dealings (158:059180) to the north of Llawhaden, so it seems reasonable to suppose that many drovers approaching Narberth market from that direction would make for the banks of the Eastern Cleddau and follow the river south to Canaston Bridge. We can join them on that part of the journey by taking the track through the woods, winding down towards Llawhaden church from the castle ruins.

But first you will want to spend some time looking at this fortified residence of the Bishops of St David's. To my mind it is one of the most romantically sited and sensitively preserved of the castles of south Wales, comparable only to that of Cilgerran which we shall visit during the course of the walks in Chapter 4. Llawhadan dates mainly from the fourteenth century, but there was certainly a castle on this site two hundred years earlier when Giraldus Cambrensis, who had hopes of becoming Bishop of St David's himself, came here on a visit to his uncle who held that see.

Dii The walk south from here goes through the settlement of St Kenox, where it is possible to cross the river and make for the lane going down to Robeston Wathen. If you keep to the west bank you come to Canaston Bridge. Both routes faced the cattle drovers with unavoidable toll gates before they could get to Narberth: a predicament that those who went south of the Haverfordwest/Whitland highway were able to escape. Let us look at their routes, starting from the footpath that goes south round Arnolds Hill to the farm of Hillblock and then east past Cresborough and Coldblow to the lane leading up to Slebach House and Park.

Slebach Forest, noted by Charles Hassall in 1794 as being 'the most considerable wooded estate' in Pembrokeshire, extends along both banks of the Eastern Cleddau. If you go down to the water before entering the trees you will find a ruined church dedicated to St John (158:032139), a reminder that the Knights of St John of Jerusalem founded a Commandery here in the twelfth century. The church stands across the river opposite the shell of a great barn, part of a complex of buildings mentioned as the Sisters' House by Richard Fenton in his 1811 *Historical Tour through Pembrokeshire*. The path through the woods here leads to the crossing of the river by Blackpool, which once served as a port for water-borne produce. The mill stands on a site where wood from Slebach Forest was used to fire an iron forge producing agricultural and domestic equipment. Those workings, started in the sixteenth century, grew into an enormous concern owned by the Carmarthen Iron Works. In 1792, the firm produced an industrial token bearing an image of the interior of the forge. It shows the smith standing by the furnace; he holds the red-hot iron on an anvil, placed beneath a massive water-powered trip-hammer. In 1813 the present mill was built to grind corn; now its main business is the café, which will fortify you for your woodland walk east to a crossing of the A4075 and the path going round the northern edge of Canaston Woods to the lane running past Returno Farm. If you take the footpath north from here, you will find a river crossing, which leads to the path going into the centre of Narberth. This route avoids Narberth Bridge, where a heavy toll was charged after the main road from Whitland (now the B4315 through Coldblow and Tavernspite) was turnpiked in 1771. If you want to look at Narberth Castle, however, you will do better to carry on east from Returno Farm for the best part of a mile, before crossing the river for the path that leads towards the thirteenth-century tower of St Andrew's church. You will still have avoided the bridge.

Narberth castle is not at present open to the public; a mass of crumbling stonework is all that is left of the 'little preati pile' which John Leland admired when he came here in the 1530s. It has been long decayed; a survey of 1609 claimed that it had been 'wasted for at least twenty years'. So the ruins we see today would be familiar enough to the drovers, although their main interest would more likely have been in the Rutzen Arms, built in 1833 by Baron de Rutzen. It stood on the site of the present Rutzen Hotel, put up in the early years of the twentieth century to take the place of a small coaching inn, where Nelson stayed during his tour of Pembrokeshire in 1802.

As such it must have been well known to the drovers and cattle dealers who came to the fairs, which were held quarterly in the town from 1792, and eight times a year after 1850. By 1890, the fairs were being held monthly, when some seven hundred cattle, a hundred and fifty sheep and about a hundred pigs could be herded into the wide streets of the town. To save the cattle drovers having to carry large sums of money to the English markets, the Narberth and Pembrokeshire Bank was set up in 1811. Its bills could be redeemed for cash after the herd was sold in England, each note being marked with two oxen resolutely striding eastwards. However, it was not only the long-distance drovers who were concerned with the animals coming into Narberth market. Local farmers would bring livestock in regularly, and in the late nineteenth century children were given days off school to drive sheep and cattle into the town from the surrounding villages.

By 1839, as we shall see when we visit Efailwen in the last walk of this

Ruins of Narberth Castle.

chaptor, the heavy tolls along the main routes had become such an affliction to drovers and farmers alike that many men in south Wales took direct action against the toll gates. Taking inspiration from *Genesis*

24,v,60 'And they blessed Rebekah and said unto her, Thou art our sister, be thou the mother of thousands of millions, and let thy seed possess the gate of those which hate them,' they set about a campaign of intimidation. Calling their leader Rebecca and disguising themselves in women's clothes, their horses being covered with white sheets to avoid recognition, they mounted attacks on the iniquitous toll gates. They came to Narberth in 1843, and in a quarter of an hour destroyed the gate on Narberth bridge and the one leading to the Whitland road.

E Now I should like to look at the routes taken by the herds being driven into Narberth from the north. I shall start from the lane going east out of the village of Maenclochog (158:084274), the site of important cattle fairs. When the lane branches, take the right-hand fork for about half a mile until you come to a footpath heading south-east. This will take you across a strip of woodland, past Blaenilwydarth Farm to Blaen-sawd and the farm-track that will bring you on to the lane next door to the solitary, trimly thatched cottage of Penrhos, now run as a museum housing the traditional Welsh furniture left by Rachel and Maria Williams, the last people to live here.

This building is said to stand on the site of a 'moonlight house', a *ty unnos*, so-called because it was built in one night, in compliance with a long-standing local law that decreed that any building put up in that space of time and showing smoke coming out of the chimney (or hole in the roof) by sunrise could be lawfully occupied by the builder, who would have rights to some of the land around it. A poor smith is supposed to have built Penrhos in March 1790. His work lasted sixty years, the present house having been set up in its place in the middle of the nineteenth century.

Across the lane from the little museum, a path goes over the hill to the Eastern Cleddau. Cross the lane to the path leading to the bridge north of Alltypistyll, then turn south along the east bank of the river to Llethermadin. Turn east there and almost immediately follow the foot-path over the hills to the old coaching inn on the A478. To the south are the villages of Llandissilio, Clunderwen (from which the cattle were later to be taken to the east by train), and Caermaenau Fawr. The latter was the site of a smithy where hundreds of cattle were first shod for their two-month journey to the east.

Any herds being taken to Narberth along that route would be subject to unavoidable tolls; and we shall start the last walk of this chapter to the north, on the same main road, at the village of Efailwen (158:134254). It was here that Rebecca first roused 'her' troops to rebellion by burning the toll gate late on the evening of Whit-Monday, May 13th, 1839. The attack was led by red-headed Thomas Rees, who had spent the previous day reciting the catechism at Bethel chapel in his home village of Mynachlog-ddu, a performance which had more to do with establishing his leadership than confirming his piety.

We shall visit the *ty unnos* that he set up when we look at that area of the Preseli Hills in Chapter 4. At Efailwen, a plaque on the main road records his attack; it was put up in 1964, and unveiled by the historian, David Williams. It shows Tom Rees mounted, berobed and flourishing an axe as he leads the charge against the hated gate. His story is told in Welsh, carved in clear letters beneath the engraving. After that one spectacular protest, Tom Rees seems to have lived a peaceful life, until the age of 70, when as his tombstone by the Bethel chapel records, he died suddenly in 1876 when fetching a cabbage from his garden for his dinner. Rebecca made history without him.

The wide verges of the lane running north-east out of Efailwen confirm that this was once a drove, and one that I shall have reason to comment on later. The drovers taking the cattle south to the Narberth markets had several tolls to avoid along the main highway, and so may well have taken the parallel route going south from Login on the banks of the Taf to Llanddewi Velfrey, a place we shall look at in Chapter 2.

F There are two ways of reaching Login from Efailwen. One leaves the village by the lane running to the south-east and starts along the farm-track to Rhosfach (158:145255). Here you will find a field-path running above a wood to Llandre (158:154234). Since much of this path across farmland is not always easy to negotiate, an alternative route, which will involve you in far less hassle with blocked hedges and field boundaries, takes you across the wooded valley by the path that goes from March-gwyn (158:152245) to Pantyrodyn (158:154250). Turn right here, walking along the hillside to the next farm (Penrallt), where you will find an old overgrown track, thought to have once been a drove, which goes down into the valley and beside the stream to Login.

The alternative route to Llandre goes from the other side of the lane linking Efailwen to the Taf. The path, which goes across farmland and is sometimes in dispute, starts from the south of Efailwen (158:134253), being a continuation of the minor road leading through the village from the A478, and then runs almost parallel to the lane until it comes to Jacob's Well (Ffynnon Iago), where it joins the lane running north-east to Llandre. If you want to make a circular walk here, you can turn right along the lanes from Login and then go north by the western banks of the Taf to Bachsylw (158:165257), and turn west along the farm road to Pant-y-Caws on the drove going north-east from Efailwen.

circular

The old smithy at Llanboidy.

The route south from Login towards Narberth goes by lanes to Llanddewi Velfrey on the A40, but those herds that were not being driven to Narberth would have been taken to the east across the river from Login towards Llanboidy, an important gathering centre, naturally protected by toll gates. It might have been possible to avoid them by going along the valley to Maesgwynne, although that would only have been feasible in dry weather. To follow that way, take the left-hand fork after crossing the bridge at Login and almost immediately you will come to a woodland path on your right. You will have to persevere through some new forestry planting as you follow the stream to a meeting place of old routes, where traces of a prehistoric settlement indicate that these tracks across the hills have been in use for thousands of years. Take the one that goes north to a crossing of the stream and then follow another, along the valley to the east, when your way will soon become clearer. The path by this second stream brings you round the edge of a hill to a lane. Take it, in order to cross the water, and then continue along the south bank of the stream to the pool, which forms its source.

The path now continues to the north of the wooded parkland of Maesgwynne, where another toll gate barred the way to Llanboidy a mile or so to the south-east. The path takes you past the ruins of the great house of the Powells, now completely neglected. There was once an idea of turning it into a hotel, but it never materialized.

Possibly there was a way of avoiding the Maesgwynne toll by going south-west from the park gates towards Crosshands and taking the farm road from Maesgwyn Isaf near Blaencwmmau (158:203229). From there a path goes steeply downhill to the valley, a descent that many drovers might find hard to negotiate. If they managed it, it would bring them into Llanboidy by the lanes at the back of the village.

Llanboidy's droving connection with London's Smithfield (the term for a meat market also widely used throughout Wales) is still remembered in the open square, which is called Piccadilly. For although most of the cattle being driven out of Wales were destined for English grazing grounds before they were finally sold for slaughter, London was the goal of many Welsh drovers, and several of them got there, spending days in Shepherds Bush before returning to the West. Llanboidy, itself, was one of the most important collecting centres for cattle in the south-west, and many drove routes diverged from it. To the north, the way ran past Cwmfelin Mynach, which derives its name from the mill set up by the monks of Whitland Abbey. The Drovers Inn, however, is a more recent, and to us more pertinent testimony to its history. It marks the routes that the droves took through Blaenwaun (158:236273), where the herds would be joined by those going directly east from Efailwen along the lane

Along the path from Llanboidy to Bancyllain.

that we noted when we started out from that village. To the east of Llanboidy, the route went through Meidrim to St Clears. We shall follow that way to the south, going to Whitland, where these cattle would be joined by the herds coming out of Narberth. In fact this latter route could well have served as a drove in both directions, as some of the herds from Whitland might have been driven north along it towards Newcastle Emlyn, in which case they would have been shod at the smithy at Bancyllain.

Two other shoeing stations have been listed in this area by Richard J. Moore-Colyer in *The Welsh Cattle Drovers* (University of Wales Press, 1976). One was at Caerlleon (158:257220) by the crossing of the Cynig on the way to Meidrim; the other was actually in Llanboidy at Waun Rhiwan. The route that the droves took south out of Llanboidy is the old road that runs by the Afon Gronw just west of the smithy (now a pottery) on Haford Hill (158:218227). This makes a delightful but somewhat overgrown valley walk, which enters a wood, crosses the Gronw and comes out past the vestiges of the lost village of Cilhirwydd at the old shoeing station at Bancyllain, a place which continues its association with long-distance routes by serving as a coach and lorry park. The numbers of shoeing stations around Llanboidy indicate the vast numbers of cattle that changed hands here and started out on the routes to the east.

It is possible that the toll gate to the east of Whitland could have been avoided by taking the old route through the southern part of the Gronw valley, a way that goes past the meagre ruins of Whitland Abbey. They mark the site of the first Cistercian foundation in Wales, set up in 1140 in a wooded area described by Leland in the sixteenth century as a wilderness. In all probability this is also the site of the White House, where King Howell the Good (Hywell Dda) called his wise men together in 930 AD in order to codify the laws of Wales.

To reach the abbey ruins, leave the lane a couple of miles south of Bancyllain at Llangoli (158:215184) and take the path going down through a wood to a river crossing. The abbey ruins are on the western bank, and the lane going from them, back across the river to the south, will take you almost into the centre of the town, where you can learn more about Hywell Dda in a small modern museum set in a little formal garden adorned with tiles on which the laws are inscribed, properly in Welsh. You will find the English versions set out for you inside.

If you do not want to go into Whitland itself, you can follow the route of those drovers who were heading for St Clears and who may well have cut out some of the tolls along the highway managed by the Whitland Trust by taking the hill-top path which leaves the lane from Bancyllain at 158: 222189 by the farm-track to Pantygrug.

The path to the south here goes through the fields of Tafan y Wanoc to the west of East Regwn Farm, whose access road brings you on the main road about four miles to the west of St Clears. The story of the journey going east from there, and the route that drovers took to the south of the main highway is described in the next chapter.

Riding Stable
Eric and Sue Scourfield
Pennybridge Farm
Hundleton
Pembroke
Dyfed SA71 5RD

Chapter 2

To St Clears and Carmarthen

I will describe the route to St Clears beginning with the southern route from Narberth to Whitland, going past the farms to the east of Narberth that stand out on the hillsides on either slope of the wide valley of the Marlais River. It is here that the B road runs through Tavernspite (158:182128), a way that was barred by toll gates. So it makes sense to look at the lanes and by-ways running to the north of it.

Here you are well away from Pembrokeshire's main tourist area, there is no dramatic scenery, no outstanding prehistoric or medieval monuments, simply the signs of a long history of agriculture among pleasantly wooded hills. The tracks we shall walk along in this region were used by the earliest stock-breeders, who built their forts and enclosures overlooking the west/east valley.

A From Narberth a lane goes directly east to Lampeter Velfrey, birthplace of the archaeologist Glyn Daniel: a good region to explore, but one that we shall approach more indirectly. The cattle that were shod at Caer-maenau Fawr probably started their journey to the east by going uphill along the path that branches off from the high road, now the A478, at 122164. If you follow that route you will come to a lane that leads to a footpath running between the two hill forts of Caerau Gaer and Llanddewi Gaer on the hill above the Afon Marlais to the south of Llanddewi Velfrey. From here you go downhill to the river and the lane that goes under the railway line to Tygwyn Farm (158:164145) and the uphill path to the east of Lampeter Velfrey. There was a local tradition that this was the hill on which Noah's ark came to rest, and as you climb steeply towards the lane to the south you may well feel it has some basis in fact, especially when the valley meadows are flooded.

To explore the farms on the southern side of the valley, take the lane going south until you reach Gilfach farm. Here a path leads round the hillside to a narrow wooded valley, out of which a lane climbs steeply north-east, heading towards the dominant, silvery cubic blocks of Whitland's creamery and dairy plant. There is one more footpath, cutting off a corner of the lane before you make the descent to the town. It runs across the hill from 158:184147 to 158:187154.

This way will bring you to the modern bridge that carries the traffic across the river into Whitland. The old bridge by St Mary's church on the other side of the river still exists, although it is blocked at its southern end; a footpath between that bridge and the church goes through fields and across the railway line to join the A40 opposite the path to Whitland Abbey (see Chapter 1).

However, the droves heading east would stay to the south of the Taf in order to avoid the toll gate at Pwll-Trap to the west of St Clears. That is a built-up area now, and one which you too will be glad to avoid. So do not cross the river into Whitland, unless you have not already had an opportunity to visit the excellent Hywell Dda centre and gardens, for the route now lies south of the Taf going through the industrial estate to the east of the B4328.

Bi At Great Pale (158:223158) there is a choice of routes to St Clears. The first goes round the hillside towards Little Pale (158:235154) and then

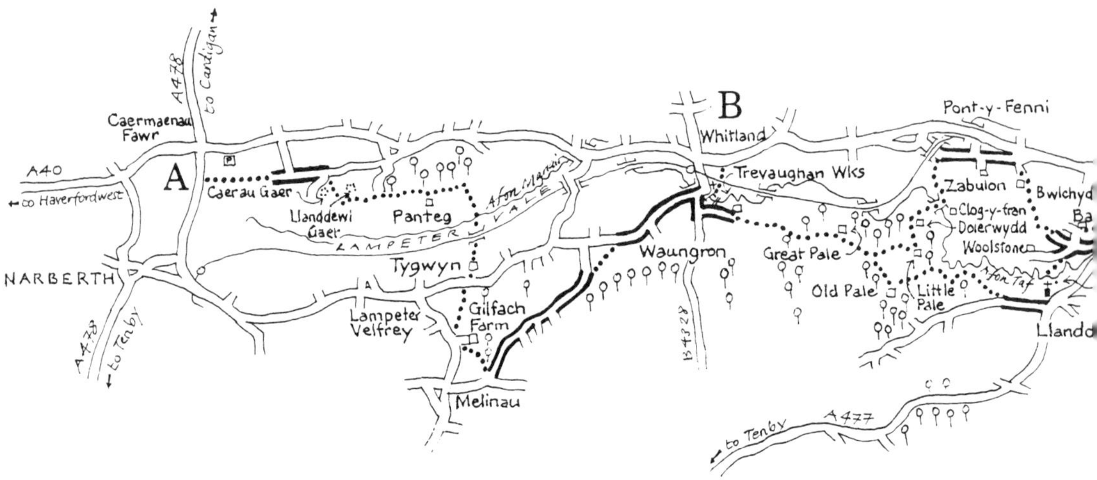

curves north to cross the river by the farms of Dolerwydd and Clog-y-fran. Take the farm road north from here and then turn east along the lane, leaving it before it reaches the A40, by taking the path going over the hills by Bwlchydomen (158:252166), and then across the valley towards Backe (158:261157) and the path that runs just north of the lane towards the A477. This route brings you out just south-west of the enormous roundabout that enables present-day traffic to by-pass the little, divided town of St Clears.

Bii The other route from Great Pale takes the path climbing through the woods to Old Pale, and then zig-zags back through the trees, going steeply downhill towards the river before turning south-east to Llanddowror.

Griffith Jones was the minister here in the first part of the eighteenth century. He was one of the most original of the great pioneers for universal education, organizing circulating schools, which toured isolated villages. Each 'school' was in operation for some three months, during which time the teachers set people of all ages, including six-year-old children, on to the path of literacy, so enabling them to have some first-hand knowledge of the scriptures. In this project, Parson Jones had the support of his father-in-law, Sir John Philipps of Picton Castle, who gave him the living of this parish.

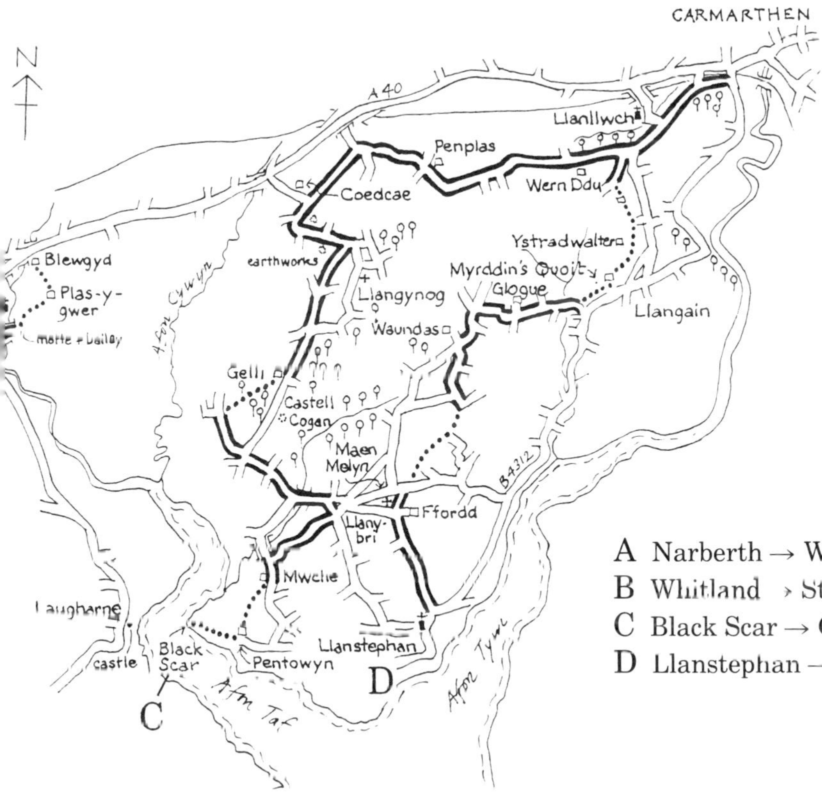

A Narberth → Whitland 10 miles
B Whitland → St Clears 8 miles
C Black Scar → Carmarthen 15 miles
D Llanstephan → Carmarthen 9 miles

Griffith Jones died in 1761, before the turnpike roads were established. However there is no doubt that he would have been familiar with the droves, which made their way past his village to the fairs and markets at St Clears. Some of them would have taken the track that runs behind the church, past the standing stone to the old ford across the Taf. That route was only passable in dry weather; when it was wet the herds would have to take the route to the north-east, crossing the river by the road that is now the A477.

If you follow that route, you will find a path heading east as soon as you have crossed the Taf. It follows the north bank of the river to a grassy knoll that was once the motte of St Clears' castle, standing to the east of the thirteenth-century church tower, built on the site of a small Cluniac priory. These historic remains flank the old town of St Clears, where the fairs and markets were held. The modern town that has eclipsed it lies to the north of the A40.

In the mid-nineteenth century, the Chartist leader Hugh Williams was mayor of St Clears and financed the building of the town hall, as well as granting space (on his wife's lands) for an enlarged cattle market. In some ways the prosperity this brought to the town made up for the iniquitous state of affairs that forced many drovers coming to these fairs to use roads owned by two different trusts, resulting in the collection of two tolls in the space of a mile.

Between St Clears and Carmarthen there is now no satisfactory alternative route to the A40, so I will now look at the way the cattle reached that market town from the peninsula lying to the south, between the estuaries of the Taf and the Tywi.

C I will begin at Black Scar (159:313108), across the sands of the estuary from Dylan Thomas's village of Laugharne, and the ruins of its twelfth-century castle on the shore beneath the churchyard of St Martin's, where the poet is buried. The area to the south of the castle is still known as Gosport, and it was from here that geese were once shipped at high tide to Bristol and the Somerset coast. During the eighteenth and nineteenth centuries, Laugharne marsh to the south was enclosed from the sea, and the sands of the estuary were used as sheepwalks, for animals who probably had to swim the narrow channel to Black Scar when the time came for them to be taken to the fair at Carmarthen.

The road going inland from here goes above the marshes to Pentowyn (159:321106). From there you can take the footpath going north beneath the hill to Mwche (159:325115) and Llanybri. Where the roads converge at the centre of that village, turn west to climb in and out of a steep valley. Then take the footpath on the right (159:141317), which goes through the woods to Gelli (159: 326148), take the lane going north-east from here towards Llargynog, and at the T junction turn left. This lane goes downhill towards the Afon Cywyn between two earthworks on the hillside. Do not go down to the river but follow the lane north-east to Coedcae (159:338182). From here you can reach Carmarthen by the road that links several hillside farms before it turns north-east to the

The castle above the sands of Laugharne.

Sands of the Taf estuary at Laugharne.

A40. If you leave the lane before it reaches the main road, by going downhill towards Llanllwch (159:385187), you will be near the field of the geese (Maesgwyddau), where the birds who were to be embarked at Laugharne had their feet prepared for the road journey. That 'shoeing' was done by getting the unfortunate creatures to walk through sand and tar until their soles were covered in a felt-like substance.

D

The second route to Carmarthen from the south starts off along lanes going north-west along the inland valley from Llanstephan to Ffordd (159:346126). Llanstephan castle makes the most dramatic beginning to this route, its curtain walls and defensive towers enclosing a rough triangular space on the flat hill-top above the west bank of the Tywi estuary. From those old walls you can make your way past the

(*Right*)
The ruined walls of Laugharne castle.

Taking the goose home from a livestock fair.

thirteenth-century battlemented tower of the parish church to the beginning of a walk that will take you past the farms whose cattle were bound for Carmarthen market.

At the old crossroads, a quarter of a mile to the north of Ffordd, take the way going straight ahead. It is a footpath climbing over a hill to join a farm road and a lane at 159:355141. Take the left-hand fork here, and in a mile or so turn right at the T-junction by the entrance to Waundas Farm (159:355152), and then follow the lanes past Glogue (159:365158) towards the B4312 and the church of Llangain.

However the route does not go onto the main road, for you will turn off the lane just after it bridges a stream and take the path going north-east across the hillside to Myrddin's Quoit (159:379161). This was a landscape known to Dylan Thomas, whose aunt Annie farmed near Llangain, and you will find echoes of it in 'Fern Hill'. The prehistoric burial mound, named for Arthur's druid, is all part of the old tradition that Carmarthen was Merlin's city, and the place of his conception. In fact it was named for the Roman garrison of Moridunum, whose walls were still standing in the twelfth century.

The way to the market town goes from the cromlech towards the farm of Ystradwalter (159:383167), whose farm road you will follow until it dog-legs to the right. At that point take the footpath going north-west towards the lane, and it will bring you by another farm road to the lane that goes past Llanllwch to Carmarthen, a somewhat forbidding town that conveys a strange bleak feeling despite all its bustling activity.

I find Carmarthen a place of great contrasts and confusing impressions, from the welter of its still active markets to the elegance of the parade and esplanade high above the Tywi. This upper part of the town is focused on the sugar-loaf civic building, a dull, impressive county hall built on the site of a prison designed by John Nash, standing among the ruins of the castle, destroyed at the time of the Civil War. You can still walk by the ruined gateway and past the few remaining stones of its walls.

In the middle of the sixteenth century, when the castle was still intact, Carmarthen was reckoned to be one of the largest towns in Wales with a population of two thousand. By the first decades of the twentieth century the numbers had grown to ten thousand and it appears to have been an enchanting place. A. C. Bradley in his *Romance of Wales* (Methuen, London, 1929) describes it as 'a fine old market town' with 'an old stone bridge of many arches crossing the tidal Tywy'. A few years later H. V. Morton writing *In Search of Wales* (Methuen, London, 1932) found Carmarthen to be 'the most vivacious market town I had seen in Wales' having 'the expression of a fat harvest-field on a sunny afternoon'. Both writers commented on the coracle fishermen netting salmon in the river; and Morton recorded their licence fee as £3.4s a year. He added that they followed a hereditary occupation in which sons followed their fathers and no interlopers were allowed to join. It is still impossible to be unaware of the river winding below Carmarthen town. The route to the east goes along it and by the rich pastures that it waters.

Riding Stable
Mrs Jackie Watson
Hills Farm Stables
Laugharne
Dyfed (099 421 375)

Chapter 3

The Roads from the Islands

Before going further east, I want to trace the ways the droves were taken through north Pembrokeshire to Fishguard and to the fairs at Haverfordwest.

For many centuries cattle and sheep were grazed on the islands off the Pembrokeshire coast and brought back to the mainland from distant Grassholm, from Skomer and Skokholm in the south, and from Ramsey Island off St David's Head. So before starting to follow the main routes to the east, I should like to spend a little while thinking about these islands — and any excuse to visit them should be seized on eagerly. The arrangements for the ferry times can be ascertained from St David's.

Although they are now mainly the haunts of bird-lovers and naturalists, they were extensively farmed within living memory, and this will become apparent as you walk across them. Skomer's 720 acres now form a National Nature Reserve with the finest sea-bird colony in south-west Britain. Here you must go carefully so as not to tread on the burrows where puffins and Manx shearwaters hide their young from marauding gulls. Then, in the middle of the island, you will come across the ruins of the farmhouse whose yards and home paddocks are now used as camping grounds for parties of archaeologists, biologists and geologists who work here in the summer.

The Celtic farmers on Skomer have left traces of their field systems on the land as well as the remains of huts and enclosures, and these can be best seen in the southern promontory of the island. From the coming of the Normans to the late Middle Ages, Skomer, Skokholm and the 21 acres of Middleholm were largely used for breeding rabbits, whose meat and skins were highly valued. Pembrokeshire's historian George Owen reported in 1603 on 'the great store of coneys' that flourished on the islands, which he noted also served as 'pasturage for sheep, kyne and oxen as well as horses'.

At that time it appeared that nobody lived permanently on Skomer, whose farmhouse seems to have been built early in the eighteenth century. In 1843, new farm buildings were put up by Charles Philipps of St Brides. He also improved the harbour at the North Haven, so that limestone could be imported to improve his pastures. The remains of two of the limekilns are still well in evidence, one forms a shelter just above the rocky ledge of the landing site, the other is on higher land above it.

The neighbouring island of Skokholm was also extensively farmed, but it is now best known from the writings of the naturalist R. M. Lockley. For twelve years from 1928 he studied the sea-birds here, farming the island and living in the steep-roofed eighteenth-century farmhouse, where students attending week-long courses in ecology and wildlife photography are now accommodated.

Seven miles to the west of Skomer is the island of Grassholm, covering 22 acres and famous for its magnificent colony of gannets. The scanty remains of a medieval farmhouse here are left to show that at one time someone lived in this totally isolated place for at least part of each year. Possibly it was the temporary home of shepherds attending the flocks who grazed here.

The sheep and cattle from all these southern islands were brought to the mainland at Martin's Haven (157:760091), the little bay from which the ferry still leaves carrying summer visitors and supplies for the nature reserve wardens.

Roscoe Howells, writer and former Pembrokeshire farmer, in his book *The Sounds Between* (Five Arches Press, 1980) describes how the cattle were brought across. They were hobbled on the shores of the islands, so that they could be laid on their sides and carefully levered onto the bottoms of straw-packed boats. Horses were usually expected to swim through the racing currents, their heads held high above the water close to the sterns of the boats. From Skokholm the cattle were also expected to swim across to Marloes Sands, a longer distance than to Martin's Haven, but without the hazard of the most fearsome current of Jack Sound flowing between Midland Isle and the mainland.

However they arrived at the Dale peninsula, the cattle from the islands were assured of good grazing there, before they were driven east through Marloes to Haverfordwest. Grass still covers more than half of the cultivated area here, and for centuries milk and beef were the main source of income for farmers, whose cattle were able to overwinter in the frost-free fields.

Ramsey Island off the northern promontory of the peninsula is the starting place for the droves that we shall follow overland to the east in this chapter. Here the stone built farm house (now used by the RSPB warden) lies in the shelter of Carnysgubor, the most northerly of the

Stone wall on Ramsey Island.

island's two hills. Our first record of the stocking of Ramsey comes from an *Inventory of the Goods of the Bishop of St David's* dated 1293. It notes that 5 steers, 8 heifers, 2 bulls, 9 bullocks and young heifers, 20 yearling calves, 44 sheep and 70 goats were all pastured there. By 1326, when the bishop had a tenant farmer on Ramsey, rents were assessed on the claim that the island could support 10 horses, 100 head of 'great cattle' and 300 sheep. However, as George Owen observed in 1603, 'The sheep of this as of the other islands yield not so much profit, as those of the mainland, their wool being coarser and much impaired with salt water.' He added that when they were brought across the water they were so 'amazed at

Ramsey Island.

Ramsey Island.

the sight of people they run and become wild and will not be taken more than wild deer'. At that time Richard Howel of Treginnis (a farm that we shall visit on the mainland) ran a ferry carrying beasts between Ramsey and Porthlysgi Bay to the south of his farm. In addition to the 'accus-

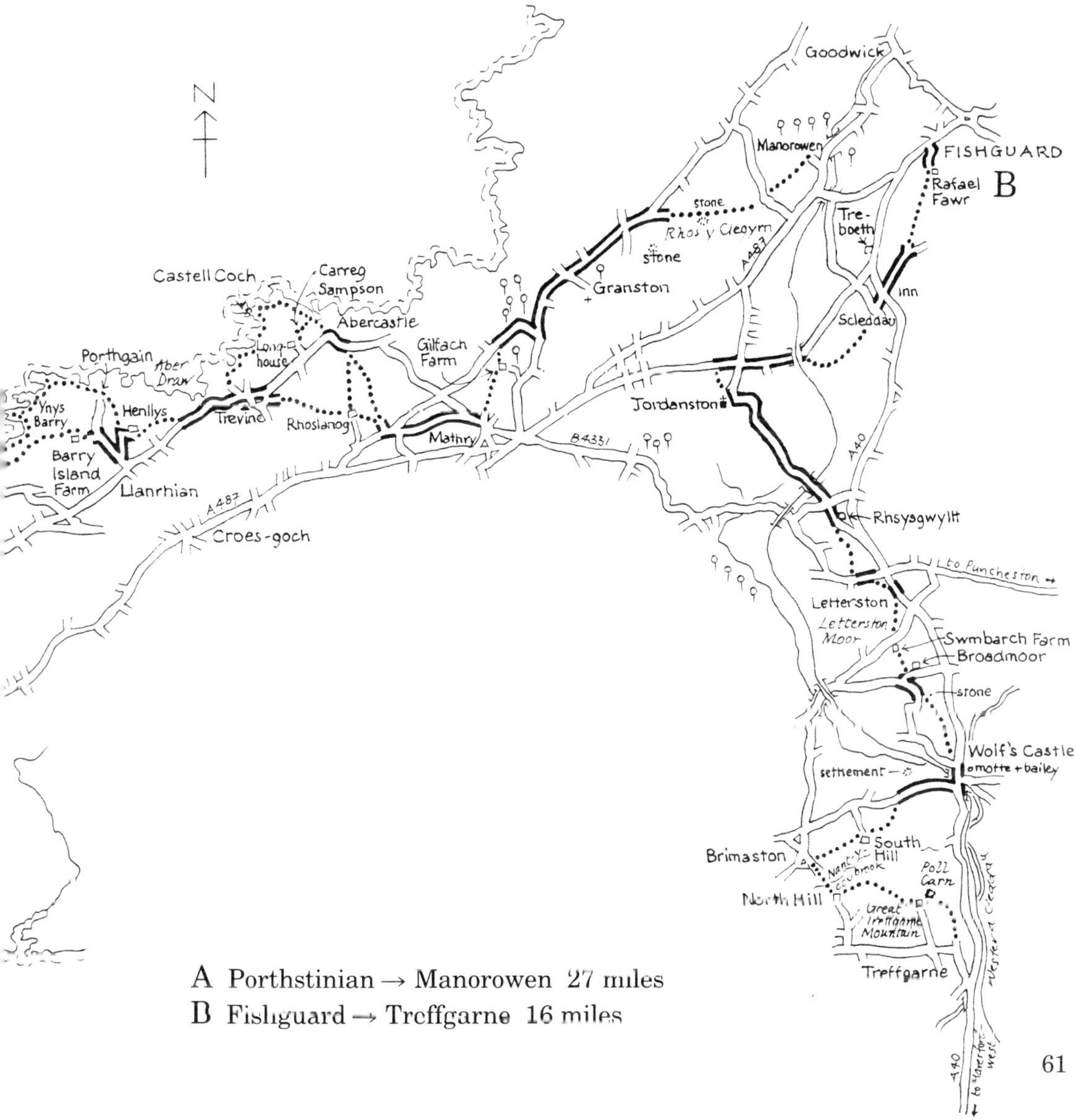

A Porthstinian → Manorowen 27 miles
B Fishguard → Treffgarne 16 miles

tomed fee' that he was entitled to charge for this service, he expected to be given two fowls at Christmas.

At the beginning of the eighteenth century, Ramsey was used entirely as pasture for horses and sheep. According to fourteenth-century records, the ewes were brought to the island from Eglwyswrw on the western edge of the Preseli Hills. So they made the journey in the reverse direction along much the same route that we shall be following towards Fishguard and the east.

A I have yet to discover when it was that the Ramsey cattle and sheep were taken to Porthstinian instead of making the longer journey to Porthlysgi Bay. The former, a rocky cove where the St David's lifeboat is now kept, is the place from which the ferry takes summer visitors to the island. It is from here that we shall start the first walk to the east, but, before setting off, it is worthwhile spending a little time looking at the displays in the lifeboat shed; they make you realize what hazardous waters the cattle had to cross between Ramsey and the mainland. It is puzzling, too, to speculate as to how the cattle could ever have negotiated the steep and slippery rocky sides of this little bay, for now a flight of concrete steps takes you from the boat to the shore. This place is associated with St David's contemporary, Justinian, who lived as a hermit on Ramsey. There is a small medieval chapel dedicated to him, standing on private ground just by the side of the lane, which can be visited during daylight hours by application to the groundsman who works here.

The cattle and sheep from Ramsey were either destined for the fair at Haverfordwest or to be driven east towards Fishguard and Cardigan. As most of the routes that they followed are now obscured by the A487, it is my intention to trace the direction in which they were heading by following the paths and droves between the farms, whose sheep may once have gone to stock Ramsey; and whose cattle may have joined the island herds on their way to the eastern fairs and graziers.

I have already mentioned Treginnis, and this is the first farm that I should like to look at. The best way to get there is to follow the narrow coastal path south from Porthstinian round the headland towards the entrance to Porthlysgi Bay. Before going inland from here, you might like to follow the coastal path above the cliffs to the narrow inlet of Porth Clais. For centuries this was the main port for the tiny city of St David's. Here the lime was brought to feed the rough pasture of this wild headland, and on each side of the narrow harbour you can still see the kilns that were in use for lime-burning between 1650 and 1900. A lane goes from here above the green pasture of the aptly called Merrivale, which is still grazed by a herd of black cattle.

Porthstinian lifeboat station.

The route that I want to take now, however, goes inland from Porthlysgi Bay, past Porth Henlys house towards Lower Treginnis Farm, which stands on National Trust land and which is used by an organization providing experience of country life for city children. They have made a beautiful restoration of the old farm buildings and dovecote, as well as adding classrooms and dormitories that actually manage to

(*Left*)
Limekilns at Porth Clais.

(*Right*)
At Lower Treginnis farm.

enhance the character of the site.

From here a sunken lane runs north-east, its banks rich with red campion, scabious and a sort of yellow vetch that I've not yet identified. This lane brings you to the camping and caravan site, working farm and home pastures of Upper Treginnis. Follow the lane from here a little way towards St David's and then turn left to cross the marshy outcrop to the west of the curious rocky outcrop of Clegyr-Boia. In this area archaeologists have made a reconstruction of one of the simple huts put up by the neolithic farmers who came to Pembrokeshire over five thousand years ago, manoeuvring their coracles north from the Bristol Channel and probably making their landfalls at Porth Clais. Excavations show that they inhabited a wooden-roofed dwelling set between walls of rock and supported by eight heavy posts. Probably they were the first people to graze cattle on this headland.

The rocky outcrop beneath which they farmed was to become the source of early Christian legends. The tradition grew up that Boia, a heathen, Celtic chieftain, attempted to lure St David into sin by having girls dance naked on these rocks, where the holy man would be sure to see them.

From here the track to the north brings you to the lane that runs west towards Porthstinian. Follow it for a little way in that direction until you reach a lane on your right. It runs past the farm of Treleddyn and

Lower Treginnis Farm.

continues towards the B4583. Turn left along that road for a quarter of a mile or so and then, before reaching Whitesands Bay, take the farm track going north past the two Porthmawr farms, and turn right above the youth hostel at Llaethdy. Above you is the 595-foot-high rocky outcrop of Carn Llidi, whose slopes are marked with Celtic fields, signs of Iron Age enclosures and Bronze age burials. If you climb to its summit you will usually find that on a day of any clarity it is possible to see the Wicklow hills of Ireland.

From here a path goes east above the flat lands of the interior. If you want to know how they were farmed in more recent times, take the farm-track going down to the museum at Lleihyr. It is open from April to September and specializes in interpreting agricultural practices in this part of Pembrokeshire.

On the uplands, the path goes north-east beneath the extensive rocks of Carneddleithr, past the farms of Treleddydfawr, Trelewyd and Llanferran, from which you descend to cross the narrow valley to Treleidir. A farm-track goes south from here to join the lane which marks one of the main drove routes to the east. Follow it past Waun Beddau, and then leave the lane to climb towards the coast and the farm of Tremynydd Fawr.

From here you must cross a wedge-shaped ridge into the next valley and Pwll-caerog farm. There is a choice of routes from here. One goes north to join a short but dramatic section of the coastal path, running above fearsome cliffs to pass the earthworks of an Iron-Age sea defence; the other goes over the hill to the north-east and reaches the lane leading into the former quarrying village of Abereiddy.

It is tempting to follow the coastal path from Abereiddy round the headland to the quay at Porthgain, partly taking the course of the still discernible tramway along which the stone was taken to the ships. This route will take you past the brilliant blue lagoon, a flooded quarry which has served as a snug anchorage since the quarries ceased operating in 1904. At Porthgain you will find, still beautifully preserved on the east side of the inlet by the Sloop Inn, the great hoppers in which, until 1931, stone was still being crushed and graded for road metal.

Ynys Barry, between Porthgain and the beach of Traeth Llyfn, whose sands stretch below the Abereiddy quarries, was once a real island cut off from the sea by the high land to the south, a fact remembered in the name of Barry Island farm. You can take the track running past it, if you take the lane towards Llanrhian; but if you are starting south-east from Porthgain, it would be better to keep to the eastern side of the valley, following the footpath by the stream to Henllys and making your way from there to Llanrhian, taking the lane north-east from there to Trevine. Alternatively it would be possible to avoid some lane walking by taking the path climbing north-east from Henllys, joining the lane about a mile closer to Trevine.

The direct route from that village goes across the valley to Rhoslanog, where it joins the lane that runs towards Mathry; but it would be a pity not to make a diversion to rejoin the coastal path, which takes you round a rocky headland, the sea to your left, and the pastures of Longhouse farm to your right. The main reason for taking this route is to visit the ponderously tilted cromlech of Carreg Sampson, a prehistoric monument comparable only to Pembrokeshire's much better known Pentre Ifan, which we shall pass close by in the next chapter. Before you reach this coastal monument to some Bronze Age chief, you will pass Castell

Kidwelly castle between Swansea and Llanstephan.

Coch (157:843338), another Iron Age headland fortification, comprising three acres of turf enclosed by double embankments and ditches.

As you turn the headland towards Abercastle, you will find a path heading inland towards the farm of Longhouse. This ancient farm whose name indicates that it was once a long building, sheltering both cattle and the farmer's family, once belonged to St David's, and the tithe corn was stored in its barns. Much later it was the setting for a great religious meeting attended by Howell Harris, farmer and evangelist, whose lands we shall cross when we travel east to the Black Mountains. The cromlech of Sampson stands just off the path before you come to the Longhouse. Nearly five thousand years ago these stones were covered with a large circular mound, probably adorned with white stones and pebbles, making the burial monument into an important landmark for those at sea. Now all that remains is the formidable capstone, held in place by the three supporting stones, on which the superstructure was piled. The monument gets its name from the super-human strength of the men who lifted that monolith into place. Indeed tradition claims that it was one man who did it, a miracle-performing Samson, who used a single finger for his gigantic task.

Beyond the cromlech, the coastal path runs beneath the cliffs to the narrow little port of Abercastle, going past the limekilns where stone was treated to dress the fields around Mathry, long-reckoned to be the richest farming area in this part of Wales. It is almost impossible now to imagine that the tiny, narrow inlet of Abercastle was once an important port, providing a channel deep enough for nineteenth-century trading vessels from Liverpool and Bristol to put in with anthracite to fire the limekilns (as well as with more domestic goods) and to take corn and butter back to the big cities.

If you take the lane going east out of Abercastle, you will come to a choice of paths on your right. One climbs gently to Rhoslanog, the other follows the course of a stream for a little way and then makes a more abrupt ascent. Both routes lead to farm-tracks coming out on a lane just over a mile to the west of the hill-top village of Mathry. Here, as in many other places along this coast, you will notice how the cottage roofs have been thickly grouted, a protection against the off-shore winds.

A market was held in Mathry for centuries, licensed on a charter granted by Edward III. Behind the church, set on the site of an ancient Christian settlement, a footpath goes downhill to Gilfach farm. Turn left here to join the lane which will take you into a steep and wooded valley. When you have climbed up on the further side, go north-east over two crossroads, when you will come to the track that runs due east over Rhos y Clegyrn, whose cairns and at least one notable standing stone indicate a flourishing Bronze Age settlement. Cross the lane on the further side of this stretch of ancient common land, and climb over Manorowen Hill. A short stretch of farm road by the side of a wood from here will bring you to the A487 heading for Goodwick, where the packets set off for Ireland.

To the north-east of the main road, beyond the farms of Strumble Head, is Carregwastad Point above the little inlet, which saw the last invasion of Britain, when, in 1797, the French, under an American admiral, dared a brief landing on Welsh soil.

B From those farms on Strumble Head some of the cattle would have been taken south to the fair in Haverfordwest. Pigs were also taken to the same destination for sale to English buyers, who then walked the animals to Bristol. We will follow their initial route to the south from Fishguard, as far as Treffgarne, making our way above the banks of the Western Cleddau. The Fishguard Trust, notorious for its greedy and corrupt management, imposed heavy tolls on the road which now has become the A40, linking Fishguard and Haverfordwest. So the route we shall take to the south will be historically authentic in avoiding the main road, as well as making for a much better walk.

Start off by leaving Fishguard along the A40, and in less than a mile follow the side road that leads to the bridleway going across the hill from Rafael Fawr to Tre-boeth, and then take the lane to re-join the main road by the inn at Scleddau. Here, on the night of June 27th, 1843, the hordes of Rebecca attacked the toll gate's posts and walls as well as totally destroying the board on which the toll charges were listed.

From Scleddau you can take a path across the western hill, going past the school to cross a disused railway line and making your way along the lane that goes to the west beneath the existing track. Just past the crossroads take the field path south to Jordanston and then follow the lane going south-east, back across the railway to Rhysgwyllt. From here you can take the path to the inn at Letterston, a village which, like Wiston, gets its name from a hated Fleming. In this case it was one Letard Littleking, who had the misfortune to get himself known locally as 'the enemy of God and St David'. He was killed in 1137 by the Welsh who bitterly resented this intrusion across the Landsker.

Some of the droves from Mathry, making straight for the east, would have had to pass through Letterston on their way to Puncheston and the crossing of the Preseli Hills, a route we shall look at in the next chapter. Halfway from here to Puncheston is the village of Little Newcastle, where Barti Ddu (Black Bartholomew Roberts) was born in 1682. He was to become a pirate, the initiator of the Jolly Roger, a pirate flag that got its name from his custom of dressing in red *'Joli Rouge'* when he attacked a merchant ship. He first went to sea as a lad of thirteen, and it could be that the sight of drovers, walking the cattle to distant lands, first gave the young boy his lifelong wanderlust. We know that sailors who had jumped ship often joined the droves on their way to the east, and so it is very likely that the young Barti overheard some of their sea stories being recounted on the way.

A path goes south from Letterston, heading downhill across the wooded stretch of Letterston Moor. Take the lane running north-east from here to Swmbarch Farm. Now follow the footpath south to

Broadmoor, and take the angle of a lane to its continuation to Wolf's Castle past a standing stone at the head of a valley. This tiny village was established by the Normans at the place where the Western Cleddau runs through a wooded gorge.

The Romans were here before the Normans, and if you take the lane running west from the Post Office, you will come to the site of a Roman settlement first excavated in 1806. The footpath going south-west from here takes you to Brimaston Farm; from there you can cross the valley of the Nant-y-Coy Brook to North Hill farm, and from there, if you are so minded, you can climb Great Treffgarne Mountain and enter Treffgarne past the weird, volcanic rocks of Poll Carn that look as though they were growing out of the heather. If the weather does not favour such an adventure, follow the farm road from North Hill to the lane, and then turn east to the village on the west bank of another spectacular gorge of the Western Cleddau.

South from this point there was no escaping the toll gates, nor can today's walkers, heading for Haverfordwest, find any alternative route to the A40. It is better then to head east, taking the lane that runs through Spittal to the agricultural museum in Scolton Manor Country Park, where you can learn more about Haverfordwest's fairs and markets than you could ever find out by plunging into the town's traffic.

Riding Stable
D. Llewhelin
Maesgwyn Stables
Maesgwyn Farm
Fishguard
Dyfed SA65 9PR
(0348 872659)

Chapter 4

To Cardigan and Carmarthen

Ai The cattle, including those shipped into Fishguard from Ireland, that were heading straight to the eastern markets were driven to Puncheston (157:008296), an important gathering place. The walker's best way to reach that place includes a lovely path through the woods lining the banks of the Afon Gwaun. This route will also give you the chance to go by some of the farms from which the cattle were sent to the collecting pens at Puncheston.

The Afon Gwaun flows to the sea at Lower Town Fishguard through a narrow valley carved out during the last Ice Age. Its steep slopes are thickly wooded: ash, alder and willow grow near the river; stunted oaks cling to the shallow soil that barely covers the rocks at the upper levels. It is a beautiful and romantic place, and it is easy to understand why Richard Fenton should have chosen this spot to build a house for his mistress, Eloise la Baronne Pillet de Mondon, and that his friends, Oliver Goldsmith, Edmund Burke, Joshua Reynolds and Samuel Johnson should have chosen to visit him there.

You can reach the riverside by leaving the A487 to the east of Fishguard and going south by the farm of Cilshafe Uchaf to cross the Gwaun valley past Tre-llan to the church of Llanllawer (157:987359) and its nearby well. This had the evil reputation of being a cursing well, one into which the ill-wisher would drop bent pins as he considered what bad things he would like to have happen to his enemy. A mile along the lane to the east (157:998359), there is a strange alignment of eight standing stones of different sizes. Some of them lean against the gorse of a hedge bank and are not immediately easy to discern; however they have been described as forming a miniature Carnac, and they certainly resound with similar echoes of the mysteries of ancient days, causing the land on which they stand to be aptly named Parc y Meirw, the Field of the Dead. If you choose to seek out these stones, you can continue the walk by taking the farm-track to the east by Trollwyn fach and then going south to Cilrhedyn Bridge.

Looking north from Carningli.

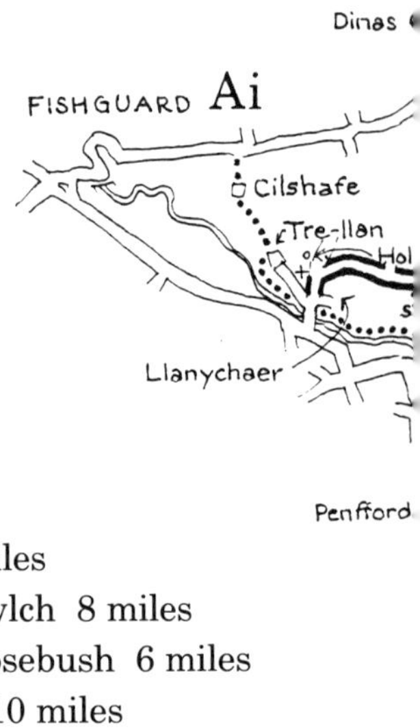

Ai A487 → Bwlch Gwynt 12 miles
Aii Bridge Farm → Tafarn-y-bwlch 8 miles
Aiii circular Preseli Ridge → Rosebush 6 miles
Bi Bwlch Gwynt → Carn Bica 10 miles
Bii Bwlch Gwynt → Gors Fawr 11 miles
Biii Ridge → Eglwyswrw 6 miles

If you are not going to look at the stones, go across the lane from Llanllawer church to the track that runs past Llanychaer court to the banks of the river. This is a place for birds. On the water, the dippers perform their curious bobbing dance on the flat rocks, and on the mountain sides you will see buzzards, ravens and redstarts, while wood warblers haunt the trees along the banks.

Whichever route you choose, you will cross the river at Cilrhedyn Bridge, and then follow the track going south, to the east of Cilrhedyn Farm and across the B4313 for the path which climbs up over bare moorland to the farm of Penffordd and the slopes of the cairn-covered Mynydd Cilciffeth, where you join the road briefly before taking the track to the left. This will bring you to a place where several tracks meet (157:017319). From here the herds going east crossed Mynydd Trenewydd and headed towards the ancient route across the ridge of the Preseli Hills.

Before following that route, you may want to go south, turn downhill from the meeting of the trackways on Mynydd Cilciffeth and so come

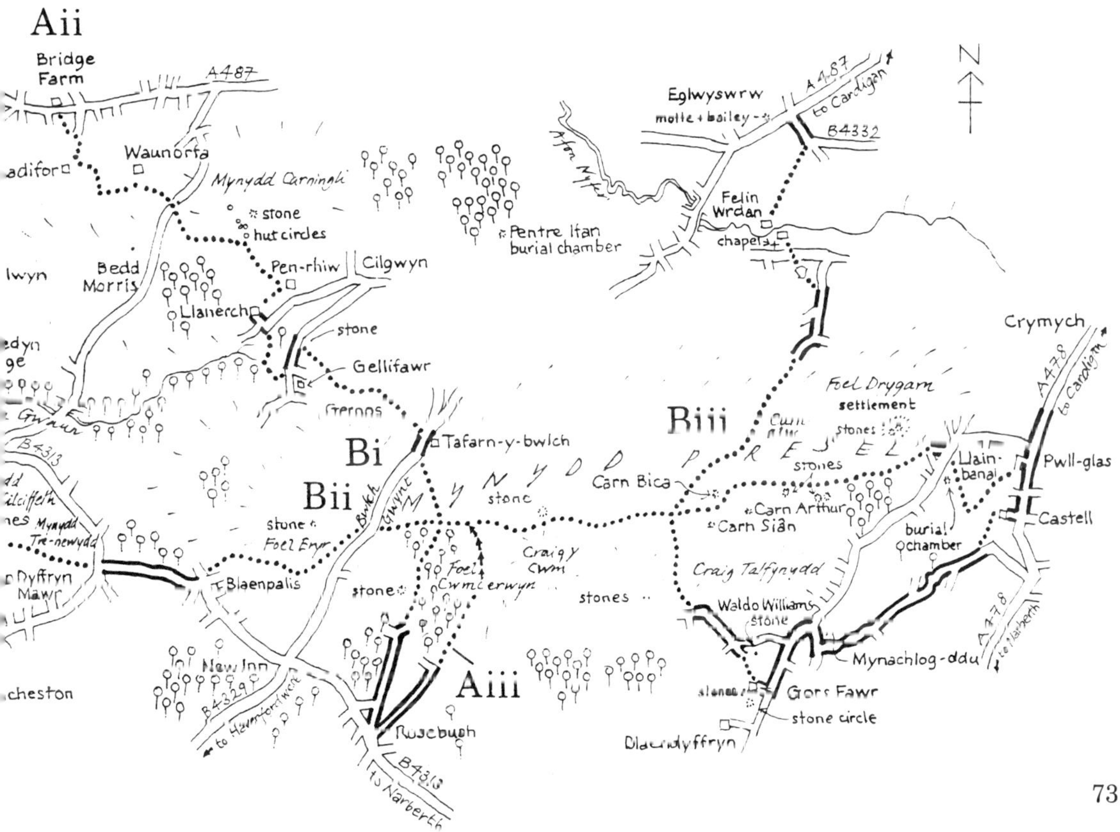

Fishguard Bay.

into Puncheston, which the Welsh know as Casmâl on account of the earthwork (remnants of a small fortification on the banks of the Afon Anghof) that you will pass before reaching the Drovers' Inn. The present name of this largish, modern village comes from a Norman knight who called the land he was granted here after his native Pontcharddon.

From Mynydd Tre-newydd the drove route joins the B4313 for just over a mile before the road makes a sharp turn to the south-east at Croes Ffordd. Just north of that place you will find the footpath going steeply towards Foel Eryr (the 'Eagle's Hill'), crowned with a Bronze Age burial

Opposite the Drovers' Inn at Puncheston.

cairn. As you take the path round the eastern slopes of that hill, you will be walking across open moorland to the pass of Bwlch Gwynt crossing the B4329 at the start of the Preseli ridgeway.

Aii It was at this point that the herds from the farms around Puncheston were joined by those coming from the farms around Newport to the east of Fishguard. You can follow their route south of the A487 by taking the farm-track that runs off the main road; go south for a couple of miles to the east of Dinas Cross. If you leave the road by Bridge Farm (145:027387) and go through the woods along the farm-track serving Trecadifor, Parke and Waunorfa you will have an idea of the steep rough pastures that the Welsh farmers 'north of the mountains' had to contend with.

Do not follow the farm-track when it turns abruptly east towards

Pentre Ifan.

Waunorfa, but take the path climbing south-east over the hill to the lane. Turn right here and within a few yards you will come to a rugged stone standing seven foot six high. This is Bedd Morris, and Richard Fenton affirms that it was here that Morris or Morus, a notorious robber, was killed by the infuriated populace. Fenton tells us that this man lived among the rocks on the summit of the hill commanding the pass that was the only road to Newport. He trained his dog to retrieve the arrows that he shot at wayfarers. There no doubt were many such characters as Fenton described in this wild area, but the stone itself was most probably set up in the Bronze Age as a waymark indicating a crossing of important trade routes. For centuries it has served as a boundary stone to mark the limits of Newport parish; what really concerns us is that the

By Pentre Ifan.

area south of the stone has long been known as the Hillock of the Cattle, and is so marked in Welsh on the Pathfinder Map (Sheet SN 0313).

From Bedd Morris, the grave of Morris, the path to the east runs across Mynydd Caregog, past the broken rocks of Carn Edward and the slopes of Carningli, a mass of barrows and hut circles culminating in a spectacular hill fort, on the other side of the valley from Pentre Ifan, Pembrokeshire's best-known prehistoric burial chamber (cromlech). Carningli, just over a thousand feet high, gives the impression of a greater eminence, partly because it supports one of the best preserved Iron Age camps in Britain, its enclosing walls being six foot high and six foot thick.

Legend has it that here the sixth-century Irish St Brynach had a vision of angels when he climbed up here from his settlement by the Afon Nyer for hours of solitary prayer. By that time the camp had long been deserted, but it was probably occupied up to the time the Romans left, and could have supported at least 150 people.

There is a grassy track heading down the steep scree-covered slopes to the east of Carningli; but the best route goes south-east from Carn Edward to Pen-rhiw and a return to the woods of the Gwaun valley. When you meet the lane at Llanerch (145:057354), you can make a diversion to Pentre Ifan by following the lane north-east to the church of Cilgwyn (145:075360). Here there are a few scattered farms, and you will find further Bronze Age stones as you take the path to the south of Carnedd Meibion Owen and then climb to the great cromlech itself, which has fascinated antiquarians since George Owen made a plan of it in 1603.

The lane that goes east through Cilgwyn leads towards Eglwyswrw, where important cattle fairs were held from the sixteenth century. Two hundred years before that, the manor was held by David Martin, bishop of St David's, who lived in a moated court house overlooked by the Norman motte, possibly on the site of the present-day Court at 145:136394. The circular churchyard of St Wrw indicates that there was a Celtic settlement here long before either of those feudal buildings was erected. At the crossroads, the Serjeants Inn is probably a reminder that this was once also a medieval armoury.

The main drove route that we are exploring from Llanerch runs to the south of Eglwyswrw along the ridge of the Preseli Hills. To reach the start of that journey from Llanerch, take the path through the woods to the lane by the farm of Gellifawr (145:062346) and then go south-east until you come to a farm-track running by a stream to Gernos Fawr, and the old road that goes across the hills to Tafarn-y-Bwlch, the site of a coaching inn, familiar to the drovers going to or coming from Eglwys-

(*Right*) Carningli from Nevern.

wrw. From here they could look south-east to the eight-mile ridge which forms the main dry route to the east. The land to the east of Tafarn-y-Bwlch itself is a watery place, unsuitable for cattle droving but pleasant enough for walkers who can enjoy the masses of forget-me-nots growing in the marshy ground by the streams.

From here you must follow the B4329 to the south-west for about half a mile in order to set across country to the Golden Road, so-called because it was a major part of the Bronze Age trackway heading for Whitesands, near St David's, and the ancient trade with Ireland. Of later years this ridge was known as the Flemings' Way, because, as George Owen explained, these unpopular incomers to Pembrokeshire could 'make this unusual way for their passage, for that passing along the top of the highest hill, they might the better descry the privy anbushes of the country people'. By Owen's own time the Preseli ridge was 'clean out of use'; and it was the coming of the toll roads that was to send some of the droves along this toll-free route.

Aiii circular

Before you follow this eight-mile walk to the east, you might like to cross the ridgeway and make a diversion south to the quarries of Rosebush, and to one of the more bizarre areas of Pembrokeshire's recent history. If you have been following the first walk over Foel Eryr to Bwlch Gwynt then you must follow the ridgeway track through the woods until you come to the path going south. This patch of hillside does not get its name from the flower, but from the Welsh *rhos* (moorland). Nevertheless the late nineteenth-century developers who hoped to turn the area to the south of the quarries into a fashionable holiday resort must have hoped that the visitors would be enticed to stay in the curious, corrugated-iron hotel by the charming rural associations of the place's name. The idea of the venture inspired Sir Hugh Owen, the local squire, to imagine that by attracting tourists he could make a double use of the railway running over his land to serve his quarries.

The quarries produced a delicate, deep blue slate, and you will see signs of them, as well as of the old railway, when you have got clear of Pantmaenog Forest. The quarries closed in 1906, but the railway was not finally lifted until 1952. The path through the trees brings you out onto the quarry road, where you can find tea at the Post Office past the terrace of old cottages that once housed the quarry workers. Cement-grouted roofs, in the traditional Pembrokeshire way, protected these dwellings from the rough weather of this moorland area and made them far more attractive than the sadly decayed glory of the hotel, just around the corner - a dilapidated dream.

From here you can return to the ridge by climbing up to Foel Cwmcerwyn, the highest point of Preseli, which George Owen assured his readers was 'the first and chiefest landmark that mariners do make at sea, coming from the south or south-west, and is their chief and sure mark whereby they make for Milford'.

You will start by following the old quarry track (145:074290) going north-east from the B4313, past the gate leading into Pantmaenog Forest at 145:084307 and up to the cairn-marked summit of Foel Cwmcerwyn. If you are very sure-footed and the weather is clear, you could take the path to the east of the hill. It will bring you to the dramatic cliffs of Craig y Cwm. Foel Cwmcerwyn, Preseli Top, is the highest point in Pembrokeshire and rises to 1,760 feet. There is no official path from its summit to the ridgeway, but you will find the way marked with old peat cuttings and easy enough to discern in clear weather.

Once back among the Bronze Age cairns of the ridgeway, you will be walking east below Foel Feddau past spectacular rocky outcrops. They are known as Cerrig Marchogion, the 'rocks of the knights', and serve as a reminder of the Mabinogion story about the fearsome black boar, Twrch Trwyth, who turns up all over south Wales. In this area the beast is supposed to have landed at Newport after crossing from Ireland. Arthur's knights chased him up into the hills, only to be gored by his cruel tusks at this spot where their bodies turned to stone.

A little further on, the west-east ridge is crossed by a north-south route, also used by the drovers on their way to Eglwyswrw, Maenclochog and Crymych. The ruins to the north of the path heading east are the remains of Tydfil, a hafod or summer grazing settlement, where stock owners could settle during the months when their cattle and sheep were pastured on this upland common.

From this old crossroads you have a choice of routes, you can either continue along the ridgeway to Llainbanal, or follow the drove route to the north or the south.

Bi I will begin with the first alternative, following the ridge as it curves slightly to the north past Carn Bica, a pile of disturbed stones that presumably once covered a Bronze Age burial. Soon you are back in Arthurian legend, for to the south of the ridge is Carn Arthur, one of Arthur's many graves, although this pile of stones is more likely to mark a neolithic burial chamber than the tomb of a fourth-century king. Beyond it to the south is Carn Siân, 'Jane's cairn', perched on a hill-top and said to mark the site of a chapel dedicated to St Silyn.

Across the head of the valley watered by the Tewgyll you will find the world-renowned spotted dolerite that form the rocks of Carnmenyn, where, as the old tales tell, Merlin discovered the blue stones to complete the magic of Stonehenge. Although the more far-fetched tales attribute

Gors Fawr circle.

their origin to Ireland (probably a medieval confusion with the Irish church in this part of Wales), it is generally thought that it was stones from this hillside that were carried to Wiltshire. Through the ages erosion caused by glacial action and frost has so worked on these rocks that they certainly now appear to have been quarried: an illusion that adds weight to the belief that it was Bronze Age men rather than the glaciers themselves that somehow transported more than eighty of these stones to Salisbury Plain.

The path going east from Carnmenyn takes you round the northern edge of forest. To your left as you pass another cairn you will see above you the thousand-foot-high, flat summit of Foel Drygarn ('The mountain of three cairns') which gets its name from three Bronze Age cairns inside an Iron Age hill fort, whose defensive ramparts mark out three separate enclosures. Over two hundred hut sites crowd round the slopes of the hill.

The ridgeway track meets the lane and the path that goes round Foel Drygarn at Croesfihangel (145:166334) by the farm of Llainbanal. The path going south-east from here comes to another branching of the ways. Take the lane on your left going over the hill to Pwll-glas on the A478, a mile to the south of the shoeing station and fair at Crymych, where many of the droves were gathered for their journey to the east.

Bii

This will also be your destination if you take the drove route going south to the west of Carn Siân, and keeping to the lower slopes of Craig Talfynydd. This will lead you to the lane, a little to the west of Mynachlog-ddu. However, in order to see the only stone circle on the Preseli Hills, you must keep straight on to the south when the lane takes an abrupt turn to the east. Gors Fawr circle (145:135295) is composed of sixteen stumpy stones, all under three foot, standing in swampy over-grazed moor land near a lane. Despite that unprepossessing description, it can in certain lights still evoke the magic that clings to such prehistoric, mysterious ritual monuments.

I find myself more moved by two more recent monuments. The first stands by the lane you did not take (145:137304), and you can reach it now by taking the first turn on your left as you go north-east to Mynachlog-ddu. The impressive standing stone that you find there is not prehistoric, although it could well be mistaken for a Bronze Age monolith. In fact it was set up in memory of Waldo Williams, poet, Quaker and pacifist, who lived from 1904 to 1971. He spent much of his life in this area, and loved these hills. From the stone you can look up across the valley to the blue stone rocks of Carnmenyn.

Preseli — monument to Waldo Williams.

The second memorial is the grave of another, earlier activist for social justice. He lies in Bethel chapel in the village of Mynachlog-ddu. Thomas

Rees, the leader of the Rebecca rioters, an enormous, red-headed giant of a Celt, known locally as Twm Carnabwth, or Tom Stonecottage, from the *ty unnos* that he built near Glynsaithmaen Farm, where the first Rebeccas gathered for their march on Efailwen. The site of the house he eventually built in place of his makeshift home is thought to be the ruin beside the stream at 145:119305.

Mynachlog-ddu means 'the black monastery', a name given to the place — which never had any monastic building — because the black monks (Benedictines) of St Dogmaels Abbey had grazing rights on this moorland, a concession which was handed down to farmers in the parish. It had no other religious significance, and in Tom's time, as now, the Bethel chapel was the spiritual centre of the community. Each year at Whitsun, Tom read out the scriptures here, a feat that he performed with as much exuberant panache as he was to bring to the storming of the toll gates. These chapel readings must have caused great pride and joy to his wife, Rachel, especially as he had to keep sober for at least two days beforehand.

To the south of the village, a lane goes north-east past hillside farms to the main road south of Crymych. However, if you take the footpath to your left, just past Wauncleddau (145:168314) you can go across country to Castell, a mile or so nearer the important market town, centred on the Crymych Arms Hotel. It was once a farm, and stands at the intersection of six roads along which the droves, including those from Eglwyswrw, four miles away, converged to set out south-east towards Meidrim, St Clears and Carmarthen; or north-east across the Afon Cych towards Newcastle Emlyn and Llandovery.

Biii If you go north from the crossroads (145:123324) back on the Preseli ridge, you will be following the route taken to and from the markets and the fairs of Eglwyswrw, held around Ascension Day, Corpus Christi and Martinmas. As you make the fairly steep descent among shapely rocky outcrops, keeping the cliffs of Carnalw to your right, you will find very marshy ground when you reach the lower slopes, caused by the many streams running from here into the Afon Nyfer. However by keeping well to the west you will soon find an old, dry, rutted farm-track running by a stone wall to the lane at 145:145351.

Follow that lane north for about a mile until it crosses a stream, then continue past the farm of Glynmaen on your right. Further on, after you have crossed the Afon Bannin you will see a footpath curving to the left. It takes you past another farm and on to the road opposite Bethabara, a starkly imposing chapel, built in 1872 to a dramatic height. It is a strange building to come across in this isolated area, although the farm road running north from it brings you to a more recent building. If you

Cattle at Nevern fair.

follow the track past that modern farmhouse, you will cross the Afon Nyfer, and then turn east to the old farm buildings, and the ruin of the old mill, sad romantic stones of the sort beloved by nineteenth- century engravers. You soon come back to reality, however, for the old mill road from here starts off by some fairly recent slurry; but soon you come to a clean, dry hollow-way and the track across Eglwyswrw Common to the B4332, just to the east of the church and the Serjeants Inn.

The old road from Eglwyswrw to Cardigan went south of St Dogmaels to a convergence of ancient tracks at Blaenwaun (145:161448). To reach that place, leave the A487 (Cardigan to Fishguard road) at 145:158434 and follow the green lane between the fields to a farm road leading east to an old cross roads. Less than a mile downhill from here you will come to a large graveyard dominated by Blaenwaun, another forbidding chapel. This one was rebuilt in 1855, about the same time that the only nearby farmhouse was constructed out of a block of four cottages arranged in two tiers, with an outside stairway to the upper set, in the Staffordshire mode. Perhaps the drovers brought the notion of this style of building back to their native land, for it is certainly foreign to this part of Wales.

Beside the chapel, a wide, well-cleared bridleway goes across country to join Long Down Bank, formerly the London road, running by St Dogmaels Abbey. Unless you wish to visit those ruins and their ancient carved stones (and they are well worth your time), you should turn right and climb up Long Down Bank for about half a mile, then take the footpath on your left (145:173448). It will bring you out to an alleyway running between houses to the two garages that flank the turn to Cardigan bridge.

Now I would like to turn to look at some of the drovers' roads east of the Teifi, around Cardigan itself; those leading into that market town from the surrounding farms, and those leading south towards Carmarthen. Cattle are still brought to the livestock market in Cardigan and at one time Cardigan Island supported flocks of sheep, brought to the market after they had swum ashore. You can still see the landing stage they were brought to if you walk round the coast along the path that starts from the car park behind the Cliff Hotel at Gwbert (145:158502). Since 1969, this forty-acre island has been grazed by a flock of St Kilda sheep, lifted off by air when their numbers increase beyond reason. The Dyfed Wildlife Trust has yet to succeed in its plan to establish puffins on the island by enticing them with decoys, but in the breeding season you should be able to see seals along this coast.

Ci From the Gwbert Hotel car park, you can follow the lane to Ferwig and then turn north (the lane is marked 'No through road') past a series of coastal, hillside farms, some of which, like Hafod (145:182504), now a large working farm approached past two ponds, were simply designed as summer holdings from which stock could be grazed on the coastal pastures. This farm road comes to an end by the entrance to the valley farm of Nantycroy (145: 185512) and from there you can take the footpath through the gate, across the valley and over the hill to Clos-y-graig. You will now be on the cliff-side walk to Mwnt.

There is a little enclosed beach here, a tiny church and a spectacular headland, all of which draw crowds of visitors. Happily, despite its popularity, the place has been preserved by the National Trust whose discreet tourist facility buildings deservedly won a Living Landscape Award in 1988. The cliffs here are pink with thrift, and silver weed glistens on the rich green sward (grass is too coarse a term for this turf),

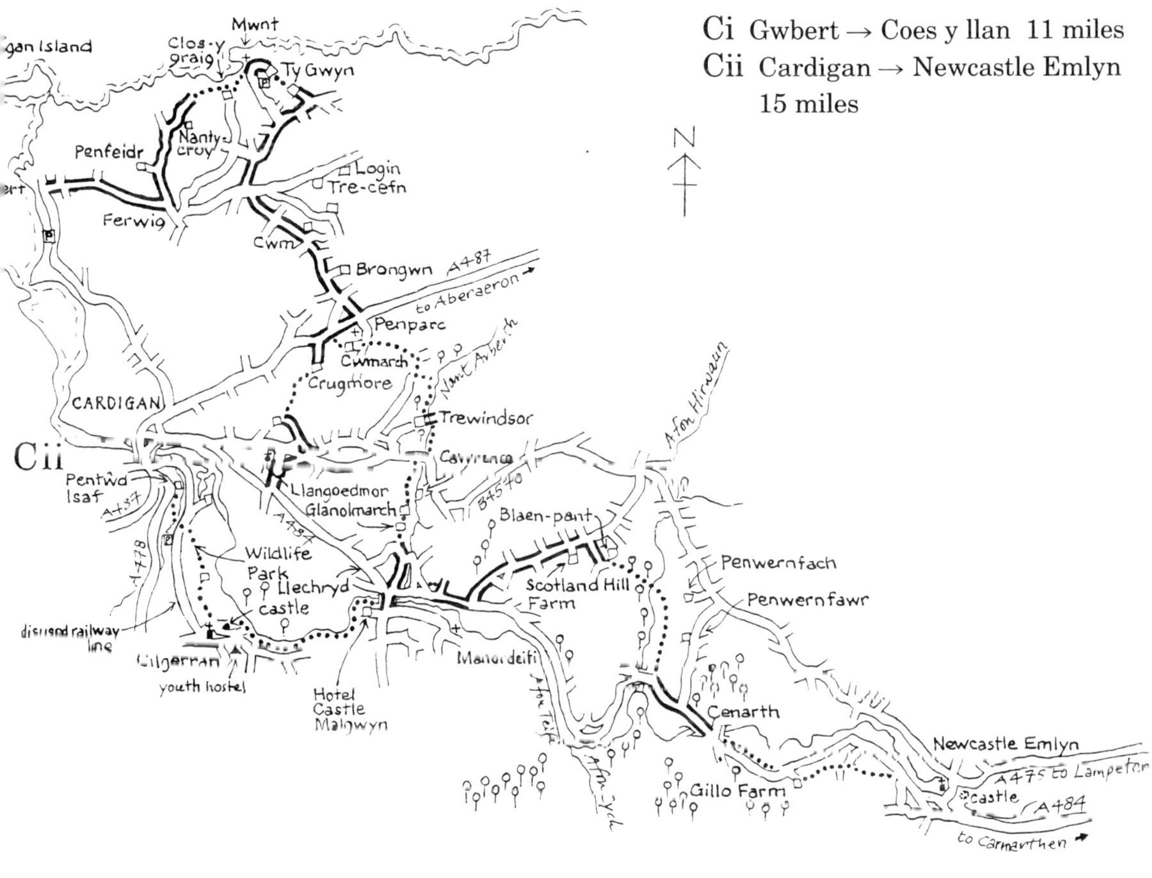

Ci Gwbert → Coes y llan 11 miles
Cii Cardigan → Newcastle Emlyn 15 miles

Poppit sands on the Teifi estuary.

which retains a salty freshness despite the hordes of summer visitors. The little whitewashed church dates mainly from the fourteenth century, although the curved beams of the rood loft were put in a hundred years later and the roof was restored in 1927. This was once a church for the pilgrims who landed here on their way to the shrines at Cardigan and St David's. A more secular sea traffic has left its mark in

The church at Mwnt.

the limekilns by the beach.

There is a path to follow past the farm of Ty Gwyn which stands to the south of Mwnt, but when you have reached the lane on the other side of the farm buildings, you will find that although the map shows a plethora of paths going towards the main Cardigan-Aberystwyth road (A487), there are actually very few on the ground. In compensation these lanes are delightful to walk along, particularly in early summer, for the fields were planted with laburnum hedges, which have now grown into large blossoming trees, so that the fields are divided by astonishing lines of waving golden chains.

If you follow the lanes past Cwm, you will join the A487 by Crugmore, a rounded knoll of a hill, dominating the landscape in an almost ridicu-

The inaccessible Crugmore.

lous way, for it rises to less than 500 feet. The hill itself is on private land, but you can take the farm road south by Banc-y-Warren Farm past Crugmore Farm to Treforgan. Turn left along the farm road here, and you will come out on the lane leading to the B4570 and the village of Llangoedmor. Cross over the B road, and head diagonally west towards the church. It boasts an endearing folly of a steeple, a stumpy, tilted spire supported by two squat tiers of four-square pillars. The lane turns abruptly here and goes downhill to Croes-y-llan on the A484. From that crossroads, you can turn right back into Cardigan or go south-east to Llechryd and the route we will be following to the markets at Newcastle Emlyn and Carmarthen.

Another and perhaps more interesting way to reach Llechryd from the

A487 is to go south from the church at Penparc to Cwmarch and then cross the lane to take the footpath that goes east through the fields to Trewindsor Farm (145:222472) and the wooded Arberth Valley. You can walk south along the banks of that stream as far as Llechryd, where it joins the Teifi. If you go that way you will have only one major road to cross, at the place where the water is bridged by the B4570 at 145:224458. Now the path goes to the west of the woods above the stream. Follow it past Glanolmarch Farm, where it becomes a lane running through the wooded valley to the east of Llechryd Bridge.

Cii One of the main routes from Cardigan to this riverside village takes you through Cilgerran, where for centuries one of the most important cattle fairs in Pembrokeshire was held around the annual feast of St Lawrence. To reach that village from Cardigan, start out above the east bank of the Teifi at Pentwd Isaf (145:183455). The path begins at the drive entrance to Pentwd, beneath the new major roadworks, and runs in a southerly direction over a rough lane, continuing across a stretch of marshy ground, bordering a disused railway track. This is not a path to be attempted in very wet weather, although much of the marsh has now been spanned by boards set above the normal flood levels. However, if conditions are right, this makes for a good walk, which will bring you near the bird-watchers' hide on the side of a small green knoll, and take you down to the little Pilliau stream, which drains the marsh when it is not itself in flood. Once across the stream you will come to the course of the old railway track, now running through a wildlife park. Cross the track and go uphill in the direction of Rhiwlas cottage, following signs pointing to the staff car park. As you go by you may glimpse red deer, Soay sheep and possibly some exotic pigs in the neighbouring paddocks.

The cottage now serves as the staff house, and once past it you can follow a deep hollow-way, a path that has been so worn down by constant use that its banks rear steeply on either side, going through the woods along the sides of the ridge separating this place from the Teifi valley. This old road to Cardigan will bring you out below Forest Farm (145:188439), once a manor house and home of Dr Thomas Phaer, a noted literary figure who died in 1560. His major achievement was a translation into English of the nine books of Virgil's *Aeneid*.

When you come to the farm road, follow it to the lane above the cottages that crowd round a swiftly flowing, channelled tributary of the Teifi, beneath Cilgerran church. To reach that church, you must follow the lane round to the right, where it crosses a stream and then climbs up to the village that stands high above the river. Once past the church you will find signs showing the walkway to the castle.

This is a romantically spectacular, twelfth century ruin, in the care of

CADW (Welsh Historic Monuments) and the National Trust who have preserved it so to stimulate the imagination of any historically atuned visitor. Even those who have little interest in the Middle Ages will be impressed by its setting, perched high on the cliffs at the tidal limit of the Teifi, where the river flows swiftly between densely wooded banks, still luxuriant although the trees have been sadly diminished during the centuries, as the sessile oaks were felled to provide ship's timbers, and the charcoal burners were constantly hungry for fuel.

One of the best ways to see this castle is from the river path beneath it. To reach it, go into Cilgerran village, a place once of enough importance to be described as one of the ancient boroughs of the county of Pembroke. So it was suitable that great cattle fairs were held in its main street. By 1800, two summer fairs took place here, in July and August; and it was in that year that some twenty thousand beasts were sold, a figure that I have from Richard J. Moore-Colyer, an historian who has done much work on the Welsh cattle trade as well as writing a book on the River Teifi (Gomer Press, Llandysul, 1987).

From the sixteenth century, wool was taken from Cilgerran to be sold at Cardigan market. George Owen recorded that these fleeces were bought by the men of North Wales 'and wrought by them to white clothes which they sell to Shrewsbury men'.

At the far end of Cilgerran's main street turn down to the river by the Post Office stores, and then for an impressive view of the gorge walk downstream towards the castle past the piles of slates left as evidence of the eighteenth-century quarry workings. Upstream the path follows the winding river to Llechryd bridge, built in 1638. In August 1843, some three hundred Rebeccas smashed the salmon weir beneath it, primarily as a gesture of defiance to Abel Lewes Gower, a governor of the Bank of England, as a way of making the Government take notice of their cause. This ancestor of David Gower, the Test Cricketer, appears to have been a very reasonable man, and *The Times* of October 14th, 1843, was able to report that he had met the people of Llechryd and agreed to abolish the weir, which had been made a symbol of contention. He lived at Castell Malgwyn Mansion which has now become an hotel.

If you cross the road at Castle Malgwyn Lodge, you can take the old roadway which goes to the ancient church of Manordeifi. It is worth making this detour, for the building is usually left unlocked, and in it you will find two box pews complete with fireplaces on either side of the pulpit, so that the local gentry could keep warm during the interminable sermons, while the rest of the flock perished with cold.

Llechryd itself was the scene of further cattle sales, which were also held at Cenarth on the next stage of our journey. To reach the dramatic

Cilgerran castle above the Teifi.

Church at Manordeifi.

river crossing in that village without walking along a busy main road, go east along the A484 until you come to the lane going north-east to Neuadd Cross. Follow it past Scotland Hill Farm, and then turn south-east towards another wooded valley through which the Afon Hirwaun flows into the Teifi. You can cross over to the east bank and then go south along the hillside to reach the main road a mile or so to the north-west of Cenarth bridge.

(*Right*) Cenarth bridge.

Here the river falls turbulently over rocky platforms, and the place has been beloved of fishermen for eight hundred years and more. In the

Newcastle Emlyn ruins.

twelfth century it was generally believed that the salmon leap was contrived by Llawdog, the local saint, some five hundred years previously. Cenarth fishermen no longer use coracles, but here, as at Cilgerran, the art of manoeuvring these frail-looking basket-like craft has not been allowed to die. Coracle races are held near Cilgerran each August; if you want to know more about the craft, you will find an excellent display in the coracle museum at Cenarth, housed in the old mill on the southern bank of the river. Tradition also has it that it was close to this mill that Owen Glendower forded the Teifi, when he set out to capture Newcastle Emlyn in 1403.

The present bridge is a restored version of the one built in the eighteenth century by William Edwards, best known for his 140-foot span of the river Taf at Pontypridd. It was he who thought up the idea of the cylindrical holes between the arches to reduce the weight of the ever-increasing wheeled traffic that the bridge had to carry. From 1802, when the Carmarthen/Newcastle Emlyn Turnpike Trust was established, the drovers had to pay heavy tolls to get to the markets and fairs in those towns. In the early 1840s, Augustus Brigstocke, parson and relation of Cenarth's squire, was urging the local farmers to submit to authority as the Bible commanded. Rebecca did not hear his pleas, and attacked the bridge on the night of July 21st, 1843.

Cenarth's blacksmiths are well recorded and this was no doubt a shoeing station for those cattle that changed hands at the Cilgerran and Llechryd fairs. In 1760, the smith was one Samuel Powell, remembered for having Daniel Rowland (leader of the Welsh Methodists) for a brother-in-law. During most of the nineteenth century, John Thomas was the chief smith in the village. He was born at the turn of the century

Bidding at Newcastle Emlyn cattle market.

and died in 1882. The last smith left in 1953, and his forge is now part of a tourist shop.

To reach Newcastle Emlyn, where we shall leave the droves on this section of the route, you should climb out of Cenarth by the footpath that runs parallel to the main road, which you will cross by Gillo Farm (145:284410). From there the path runs along the main road until it comes to a lane going south. Follow that lane as far as the old quarry, and then take the quarry road to the A484. When you cross that main road, you will come into Newcastle Emlyn by the narrow Porth Street, called for the drovers or *porthmon*.

Pigs sold at the market in Newcastle Emlyn were mostly destined for Bristol, where the re-selling price was calculated on every twenty pounds of body weight or score pound, fourteen shillings a score being considered a reasonable price in the early years of the nineteenth century. The Welsh and English drovers who bought the hogs in the Newcastle Emlyn fairs would have to estimate the weight they were bidding for.

A large Friday market is still held here, making it a place that motorists will do well to avoid; and its London House by the cattle pens recalls the ultimate destination of many of the animals who were sold here through the centuries. For some of the droves the way went east towards Lampeter; others converged on Carmarthen, going through Cynwyl Elfed (145:375275), whose Bluebell Inn was the scene of a meeting attended by over a hundred dissatisfied farmers protesting at the toll gates, during the stormy August of 1843. The Chartist lawyer, Hugh Williams, whom we met at St Clears, was in the chair.

Riding stables and bridlepaths
Dyfed Riding Centre
Maes-y-Felin
Cardigan
SA43 3DG
Cardigan (0239) 612594/613159
These stables are on the old road between Cardigan and Haverfordwest. There are bridlepaths along it, crossing the ford at 145: 168402, and joining the lane to Eglwyswrw by the chapel at Pen-cwm. This route is marked by the lone Scots pines, planted as waymarkers.

Other bridlepaths in the area
a) From Cilgerran gorge, along the banks of the Teifi, to Forest Farm 145:189439
b) A 36-mile ride along the Preseli ridge from Maes-y-Felin *via* Llanfair

Nant Gwyn 145: 164377 to the north of Eglwyswen, go to Arnedd Wen 145: 175354, north west of Crymych; and then along the ridge.

Mrs C. James.
Dolrhanog Trekking Cente
Dolvhanog Isaf
Newport
Pembrokeshire
Dyfed SA42 0QH
0239 820432
The stables are on the eastern slopes of Carn Ingli, and provide an excellent base for following many of the routes in the Preseli National Park, described in this chapter. One bridleway used by this centre and not covered in the text starts from Bedd Morris (145:038365) and goes south along the lane until the track to the derelict Pen-gegin Farm (145:034347) is reached. From here a steep track leads down to a crossing of the Gwaun, and on the further side the bridleway goes through Penrallt Ddu farmyard (145:048339) east along the drive, across the road and out onto the Preseli Mountains past Penlanwynt (145:058330) and then south around Foel Eryr.

Chapter 5

Golden Grove, Brechfa Forest and the Black Mountain

The Bishop's Palace at Abergwili stands about a mile to the east of Carmarthen, and now serves as the county museum. It was rebuilt after a fire in 1903 destroyed the 'picturesque building, conspicuous from road and railroad with its Flemish gables' described by A. C. Bradley. Nevertheless it is still worth visiting, for it houses material that relates to agriculture in Carmarthenshire from the Middle Ages, when the pastures of the Tywi valley were already renowned for the raising of livestock.

A It is not possible to walk continuously along the river banks, so I am suggesting a route that will take you to the hill-tops from which the Tywi and its lush water meadows will be spread before you. The first of these vantage points is Merlin's Hill, which you will notice high to the east of Abergwili. If you have visited the museum, you must turn back towards Carmarthen and then take the footpath (159:434211) off the A40, just east of the bridge across the Gwili. This route crosses Bradley's railroad, now long disused, goes past the sewage works, crosses a lane, and then climbs east along the farm-track by Pen-y-banc and over the hill to Pen-y-gadair. Here it joins a lane, from which in a few hundred yards a footpath on the right climbs up Merlin's Hill. It is fitting that it should boast the name of the druid, for it is crowned by the ramparts of a hill fort. They enclose ten acres, and must have served as a stockade for cattle in the Iron Age as well as containing the hall where tribal chiefs and druids feasted.

You will have to retrace your steps downhill and when you get back to the lane you can decide whether to follow the lanes to Llanfihangel-uwch-Gwili and then go south from there along the hillside past Wern-drefi, crossing the A40 at 159:494217 to take the B road to the bridge over the Tywi; or reach that point by a more cross-country route. If you chose the latter, you will take the farm-track going downhill from

(Right) Tywi valley from Paxton's Tower.

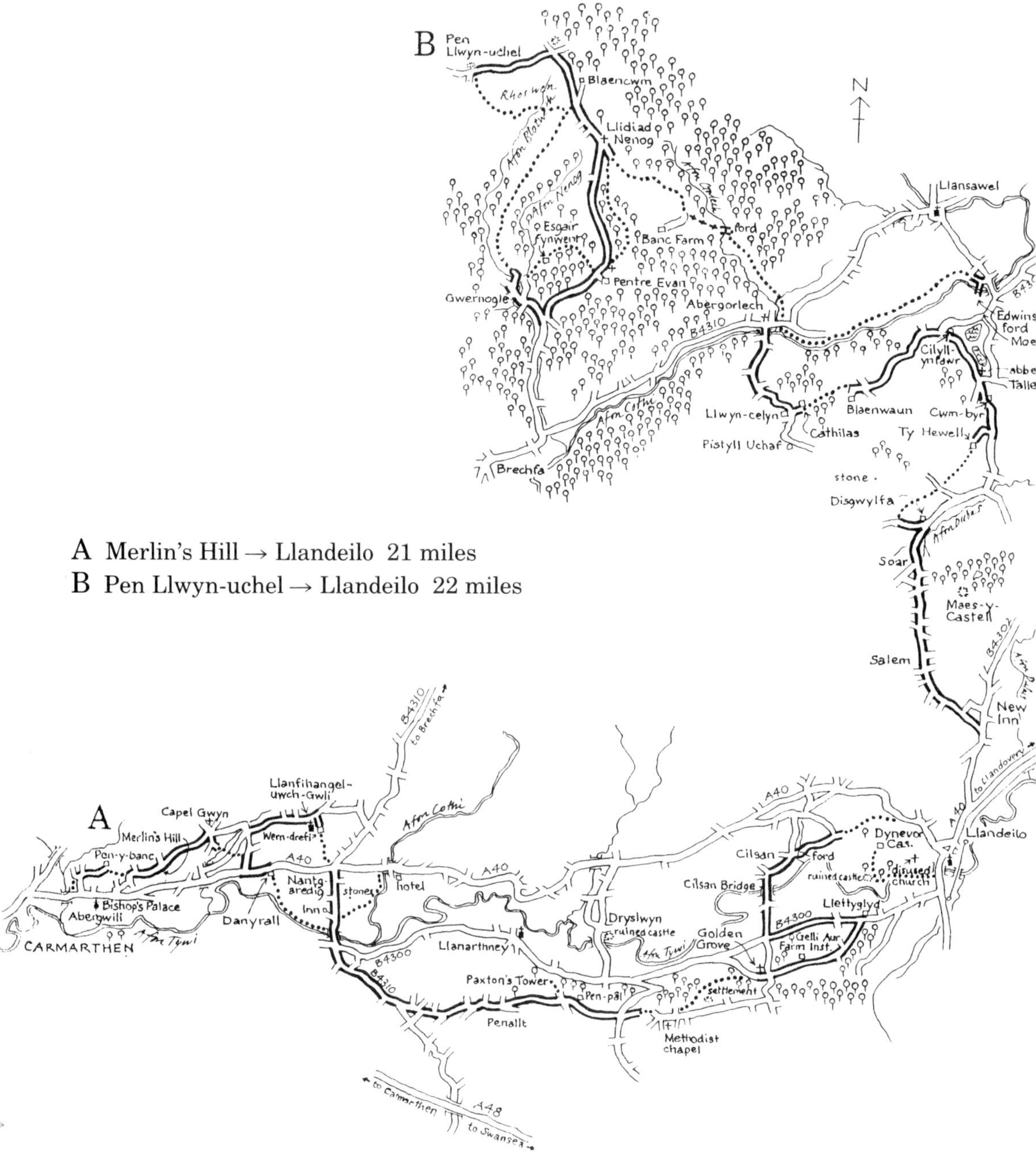

A Merlin's Hill → Llandeilo 21 miles

B Pen Llwyn-uchel → Llandeilo 22 miles

Penybanc-bach (159: 467223). It leads to a footbridge across the Annell. Climb up the hillside from there crossing over a lane. At the next lane you come to turn south, it will bring you to the A40 and you must walk along it for about a mile to the east until you come to a track running south from Danyrallt (159:478217). This track goes under the old railway line and then follows the south-eastern meander of the Tywi to the B road and the bridge across to the farms on the other side of the valley.

The next high point to the east is Paxton's Tower (159:543192). You

Paxton's Tower.

Dryslwyn Castle.

reach it by the lanes that leave the B4310 at 159:508188, and then walk over a large field to this curious hill-top folly, standing on land now owned by the National Trust. The tower, built in 1811 by Sir William Paxton, a local landowner, as a memorial to Lord Nelson, is a strange, triangular building, inscribed with dedications to the admiral in Latin,

English and Welsh. From the height on which it stands you are well above the riverside trees and can look across the water to the ruins of Dryslwyn Castle and the famously rich pastures of Golden Grove.

It is worth making the detour back across the valley to Dryslwyn. To do so you must take the B road to the north when you come to the crossroads to the east of Paxton's tower (159:558188), following this B4297 until turning right up it. The Norman castle was built on a high spur of land above the north bank of the river, and, as I write, it is still being excavated and partly reconstructed. However you can walk up to its shattered curtain walls and look east from there to the Black Mountain and the high moorland of the Brecon Beacons National Park.

When you return to the main route at the crossroads on the south side of the Tywi, you will find an unmade up road going directly east. If you follow it you will come out on a lane by the Methodist chapel of Cefenberach (159: 567188), rebuilt in 1871 but less intimidating than most buildings of that date. The wide verges of the lane that goes east from here towards the Gelli Aur Farm Institute and Country Park indicate that you are now on a drovers' route; however you may prefer to take the path that goes through the woods from 159:570187. This will take you to the lane close to Golden Grove church.

The Golden Grove estate was owned by the Earls of Cawdor, about whose farm management in Pembrokeshire the eighteenth-century Charles Hassall waxed so lyrical. In his Board of Agriculture report on Carmarthenshire, Hassall again commended the Cawdors, singling out the rival estates of Golden Grove and Dynevor as twin oases in the saddening experience of seeing 'the fine lands of the Vale of Tywi and other fertile tracts in the district, driven by the plough to the most deplorable state of sterility'. Pasture seems to have been as insensitively used as the arable ground, for he found that although the cattle of the vales were somewhat larger than the scrawny specimens on the hills, they were still 'ill-shaped and unprofitable to the pail'.

The Cawdors' last house at Golden Grove, built in 1832 and engraved with the injunction to 'BE MINDFUL', is now a college of art and technology standing in the grounds of Gelli Aur; cattle and sheep in the river pastures of its farm are in good heart. As part of the college grounds around the mansion have been made into a country park, everyone can enjoy the Cawdors' fine collection of trees and a variety of garden plants as well as the charming, wooden dovecote. Standing on the terraces you can look across the river to the rival estate of Dynevor. To get there, you can either make your way east through the park and join the farm entrance to Llettyglyd (159:611209) or go straight to the river past Golden Grove church and across the B road to Cilsan bridge

(159:589214).

Turn right here to cross the Afon Myddyfi at the site of an old ford, and then leave the lane at 159:604225 and take the footpath across the Dynevor estate. When you reach the place where the farm roads cross, turn south past the estate houses and the 'modern' castle and scramble up towards the stark grey ruins above the river (159:613217), now owned by the National Trust.

Until 1970 there was a herd of white cattle in these grounds and their ancestry could be traced back to the thirteenth century. In 1874, R. H. Harvey, writing in the first volume of the Welsh Black Cattle Herd Book, and who claimed (as we have seen) that the Welsh Blacks originated with the wild, white aurochs, commented on the fine specimens that Lord Dynevor had in his herd. 'I have often admired the five-year-old oxen as I passed the park,' he wrote, before going on to describe the finer points of the breed.

For centuries the parkland was dominated by one of the most important castles in Wales, perched high above the Tywi, and reported to have been built at the place where Hywell Dda held court. In the sixteenth century the castle was deserted for the new fortified mansion, which stands to the north and which you will have glimpsed as you made your way to the romantic ruin on the bluff.

To get to Llandeilo from the ancient castle walls, go east, down through the trees and across the riverside pasture to the woodland nature reserve and the site of the disused church of Llandyfeisant, which since 1961 has served as an interpretative centre for students of the local wildlife. The graveyard is still in use, and although the church building only dates from 1875, a feeling of much greater antiquity surrounds the dingle in which it stands and the nearby stones of a ruined house, just discernible in the undergrowth to the south. If you come here in late autumn or early spring before the naturalists get busy, you will find it easy enough to credit the belief that this was once a sacred spot to the Romans, a tradition fortified by the discovery of ancient coins near the church in the eighteenth century.

The woodland path, once the route of the old church road, widens as it goes east above the water meadows to the lane that leads to Llandeilo bridge, and the street that climbs steeply into the town. This bridge is a single-arch structure dating from 1848. A plaque on the parapet commemorates the one it replaced and which the drovers used from 1771, when the river was crossed by its seven arches. At the top of the town the four-square, plain stone-covered Provision Market is a continuing reminder of Llandeilo's importance as a market town; while the narrow Quay Street winding down to the river indicates that some of the pro-

(*Right*)
The Tywi from Llandeilo bridge.

duce was brought here by water. Although most of the cattle that changed hands at Llandeilo were driven north-east to join the herds on their way towards the Kent and Essex grazing grounds from the greater cattle market at Llandovery. However, the drovers heading to England left the mark of London names on Llandeilo, where you will still find a Charing Cross, in the same way as we found a Piccadilly at Llanboidy.

B Now I want to turn back to the north-west and explore the routes towards these markets from the farms in and around the Forest of Brechfa. To get an idea of the area, I should like to start from Pen Llwyn-uchel (146:517388), a high, desolate, flinty moorland plateau, enlivened in spring by an edging of the golden laburnum that may have delighted you around Cardigan. In wet or misty weather you might be best advised to take the lane to the east from here and then turn south to the cattle grid above Blaencwm (146:542385); but it is more interesting to reach the next point on the route by the path that skirts the western and southern margins of Rhos Wen. In its later stages, this path will take you past sheepfolds to the old road that runs south-west from the Blaencwm cattle grid. On its way it passes several isolated farms, and then goes downhill by the farmyard of Penygarreg (146:527357) to the woods that line the steep banks of the Clydach, whose waters run into the Cothi. You can follow the banks of this tributary downstream to Gwernogle (146:530340).

It is most probable that there was a shoeing station in this little village, now almost drowned by the conifer plantation of Brechfa Forest, whose cramped growths make such a contrast to the moorland heights. Certainly, cattle were shod at Brechfa itself, where the blacksmith at the time of the Rebecca Riots was one Benjamin Jones. We know about him because his sons were involved in a case of sheep stealing, accused by a crotchety, unpopular farmer; who for that and other pieces of litigation against his neighbours brought Rebecca's wrath down on his head.

If you take the road going west from the church at Gwernogle, you will go through the trees past Rhiw-Saithbren (146:525334) to join the road going south to Brechfa and the B4310, once a major coach road along the banks of the Cothi.

You can reach that road, to the east of Brechfa, by taking the lane from Gwernogle to Pentre Evan (146:548344); or by going east along the southern edge of the forest to the north of Gwernogle until you reach the farm of Esgair-fynwent (146:536345), and then walking through the trees and across the Afon Byrfon to Pentre Evan.

You may prefer the first alternative despite the lane walking, for there are more forestry walks to come, and they can easily get monotonous.

Empty house at Edwinsford.

The next one starts from the chapel at Pant-yr-Eglwys a few yards to the north-east of Pentre Evan. Here you can either choose the lane going north-east to Llidiad-Nenog (146:547375) and then turn abruptly south east at the chapel; or you can go through the forest to the cattle grid (146:557366) on the road from Llidiad-Nenog.

Follow that road over the hill-tops until it peters out by the track going south-west to Banc Farm (146:566358). Your way does not go past that farm, but back into the forest. After you have gone a little way through the trees, you will find that you can turn east to make the steep descent to the old ford across the Gorlech (146:575355) and then you can follow the east bank of that river along the forest road to the picnic site by Abergorlech post office. Here, on the steep banks of the Cothi, you will

Edwinsford.

find welcome bands of oak fringing the conifers.

The Black Lion at Abergorlech served as a coaching inn in the sixteenth century when there was a road along the north bank of the Cothi to Edwinsford (146:632345), the important crossing of the river by the main road out of Llandeilo. It is still possible to follow that old route, and it is a pleasure to do so; but if you want to see more of these hill farms you will take the lane going south from Abergorlech, climbing steeply in and out of two valleys before turning off onto the farm road by Llwyn-celyn and Cathilas (146:594318). There the road comes to an end and continues as a path which goes across a band of conifers reaching down to a narrow valley. Across the stream you meet a farm road again, and here you can climb up past Blaenwaun and the lane that leads past

(Right)
The arches of Talley Abbey.

Cilyllnfawr and then goes north to Edwinsford and south to Talley Abbey.

The abbey was founded for the French order of Premonstratensians at the end of the twelfth century by Lord Rhys of Dynevor. The two high-pointed stone arches are all that remain of its former glory and if you want to discover more of the layout of the building you must apply for the guide book from the cottage across the lane, for there is little on

Friesian cattle by Talley lakes.

the ground to help you reconstruct the past. However a path through the neighbouring churchyard beside the ruin leads down to the lakes, and it is pleasant to pause by these quiet waters before continuing the journey.

South from the ruins of the abbey, the lane goes uphill from Cwm-byr to the farm road which goes west to Tyhewell (146:632312). From that farm follow the track south-west across a valley and round a steep hillside until you reach the lane that goes east to Disgwylfa (146:624295). Before you reach that farm, you will find a turning to the south. This lane will take you across the upper waters of the Dulas, past Soar to Salem (146:623264). A little further south again and the lane forks; if you take the way to the left you will join the B4302 just outside Llandeilo.

C
circular

The final walk in this chapter will take you into the Brecon Beacons National Park. It starts between Llandeilo and Llandovery at Llangadog (160:706284) and follows two routes: one based on the old road taken by Roman soldiers, cattle drovers and the 'Cardi' carts which carried all sorts of small livestock and farm produce to the Brecon markets from the Cardiganshire farms; the other traces the fairy tale of the cattle of Llyn y Fan Fach beneath the Black Mountain.

I will start with the legend. It means taking the lane south-east over the hills for some six rugged miles, past the turnings to scattered isolated farms lying to the west of Cross Inn (160:773258). Turn south here making a steep descent to cross the Llechach in order to reach the church of Llanddeusant (160:777244). There, if you are keeping to the lane, you must turn abruptly to the east, following the route laid down for the water board to the head waters of the Sawdde. If you are using a car on this part of the route, you must leave it in the roughly made parking area just before the track crosses the river. If you are on foot, you can make an interesting diversion which relates to the story I am about to tell, if you will go due south from Llandeusant, and then turn east to the farm of Blaensawdde (160:784239) as soon as you have crossed the river. Should you continue south from the river bank, you would come to one of the wildest and most remote tracks of the National Park. It is tempting to follow it, but unfortunately it does not directly belong to this story, which is satisfactorily wild in itself, although it starts off quietly enough.

From Blaensawdde you will find a path that takes you back to the lane going east towards the parking place. Here you cross the Sawdde again and then follow its course fairly steeply uphill to Llyn y Fan Fach (160:805215). You will be walking along a fairly rough road banned to all motor transport not on water authority business. It brings you to the small dam across an ancient, natural lake. Despite that intrusion, these dark waters, whose calm can be disturbed by sudden whirlwinds, retain the magic that inspired the tale of fairy beings living in their depths. The mystery is enhanced by the wall of scree and the great, imminent back-drop of the Black Mountain itself.

The story I am about to tell has been passed down through the local families through many generations. The version I have comes from John Rhys who published it in his *Celtic Folklore* in 1901, just as he heard it from a Mr Rees who farmed at Tonn on the outskirts of Llandovery, as well as from many informants around the village of Myddfai.

The story concerns a widow of Blaensawdde, who had a son to bring up on her own. She was such a good farmer that her herds increased to the extent that she sent the boy to graze them up on the mountainside by Llyn y Fan Fach under the shadow of the cliffs of the Black Mountain. One day while he was there he saw the lady of the lake emerge from the water, and, as though she were a bird, he tried to entice her with pieces of bread. He told his mother of this encounter and twice she sent him back,

C circular Llangadog → Mydffai → Llangadog 40 miles

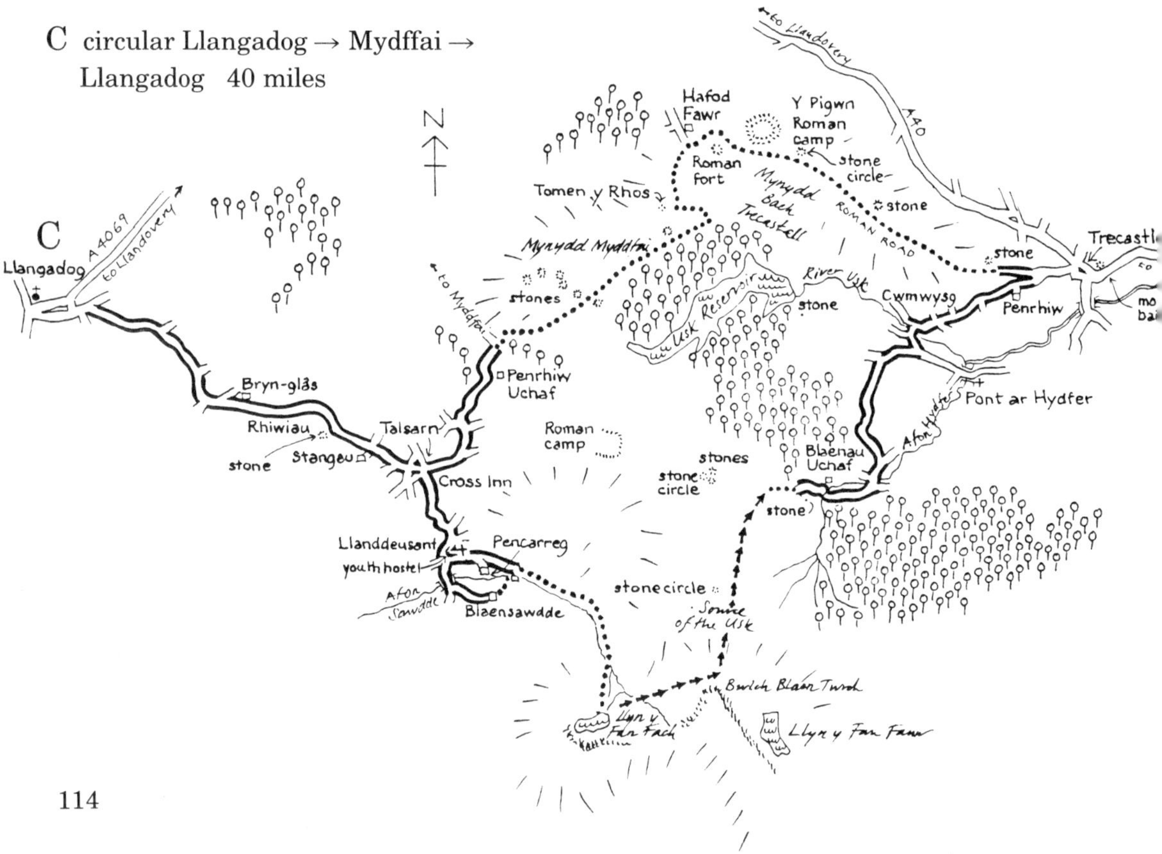

The moors of the Black Mountain.

once with unbaked bread and once with the dough half-baked, thinking that such a delicate creature would prefer something softer than the hard crusts her son took for his lunch. But always the lady glided towards the boy only to refuse the bread. It saddened him and he neglected to look after the animals, when he attended to them again he was distressed to see his mother's cattle, sheep and goats grazing on the precipitous slopes of the Fan above the water. I can understand his anxiety, for sometimes it is impossible to believe that the ponies who now emulate that feat of the Blaensawddo livestock will really retain their footholds.

Then one evening as he watched his straying animals, he was astonished at sunset to see several cows walking along the surface of the water followed by the lady. This time she took the bread he had left, and promised that she would live with him as his wife until he gave her three blows without cause. His immediate testing was not over, however, for she disappeared into the lake and when she came back to the surface it was with an identical counterpart of herself. The two ladies were followed by an old man who demanded that the youth declare which of the sisters was his love.

The boy passed that test, because his bride gave him a signal by a slight movement with her foot; and for dowry her father provided her with as many cattle, sheep, goats and horses as she could count without drawing breath. It sounds like those monstrous television hand-outs or a supermarket dash — and perhaps the tale inspired them, but these latter-day contestants for the glittering prizes are not usually as cunning as Llyn y Fan Fach's lady, who managed to increase her dowry by counting in fives.

Taking the livestock, the fairy lady and the farm lad set up their holding at Esgair-llaethdy (160:787297) near the village of Myddfai. There they lived for several years and reared three sons. The lad, now a prosperous member of the community, forgot the terms which kept his wife by his side. Without thinking, he slapped her playfully when she failed to fetch a horse from an adjoining field in order to ride to a christening. A second time he put his hand on her shoulder to comfort her when she cried at a wedding. The third time he was angry, and he struck her sharply when she burst out laughing at a funeral. At that she immediately called up her cattle

Brindled cow, white speckled,
Spotted cow, bold freckled

And the little black calf
Tho suspended on the hook
Come thou also quite well home

and back she went with her herds to the volcanic lake. She also took the four grey oxen ploughing the fields, and they left a well-marked furrow as they followed the lady the six miles back to Llyn y Fan Fach. In vain her sons kept roaming round the shores of the still waters beneath the Fans in the hope of catching a glimpse of their mother. When they had quite given up hope, she suddenly appeared to them at a place that is still known as Llidiad y Medygon, the Physicians' Gate, and there she gave

The Black Mountain.

her eldest son, Rhiwallon, powers of healing which he passed on to his descendants.

If you go to Myddfai village at the end of this walk, you will find a stone in the church porch recording the names of the doctors who kept that tradition alive. Mr David Jones of Mothrey, Surgeon, who died at the age of 61 in 1719, is remembered as an 'honest, charitable and skillful man', together with his eldest son, John Jones, who also practised as a surgeon until his death twenty years later. The last of the line of the Myddfai physicians was Dr Rice Williams who died in Aberystwyth in May 1842 at the age of 85. A medieval medical treatise purporting to come from the Myddfai physicians is held in Jesus College, Oxford. In 1861, it was edited and translated from the Welsh by John Pugh.

Now we must leave the realm of myth and folklore for the wild and trackless moor around the source of the Usk. This is not a route to be dared on your own, or in anything but settled weather, for it goes over some nasty marshes.

You set out over the wild hills to the east of Llyn y Fan Fach, walking under the cliffs of the Carmarthen and Brecon Fans that form the Black Mountain; and then turn north when you reach the springs that feed the Sychlwch stream flowing into the Sawdde. You now have about a mile of trackless moorland to cross, for you need to keep slightly to the east of the path that comes down from Bwlch Blaen Twrch (160:817218), the pass that divides the two summits and marks the county border.

You would do well to have a compass with you on this walk, and let it guide you to the north-east and the stone circle by the valley of the Tarw (160:819258). On the east bank of that river, along the southern slope of Foel Darw, you will find a path (160:829257) running north towards the forest above the Usk reservoir. Although you are not going to take this path, you should know that it leads through a conifer forest to the Usk reservoir, which drowned farms and farmlands, when it was flooded in the 1950s. There was Blaen Wysg at 160:819282, where the infant river flows into the reservoir through the newly planted conifers, and Pentre Bach to the east towards the dam. To the north, the trees of Glas Fynydd Forest, which smothers the south-eastern slopes of Mynydd Myddfai, have drowned other farms: Pen y Cae at 160:824299, a building well hidden in the trees, and Tir Cyd 160: 816287, lost beside a forest track.

However at this stage of the walk you will remain well to the south of the reservoir, keeping to the track that runs along the southern edge of the forest, crossing the river by the standing stone at Blaenau Uchaf (160:838257) and following its banks to a second crossing at Blaenau Isaf (160:846259) and the lane that goes north-east to the old ford across the Usk at Pont ar Hydfer, where there was once a smithy between the river

Farmland beneath the Black Mountain.

and the church. There is no way of crossing the water at this place now, so you must turn north-west along the lane to the bridge by Cwmwysg (160:854284) and follow the lane over the hills towards Trecastle, and the start of the four-mile stretch that carries the historical weight of this chapter.

For this was the road along which, in early winter, farm produce was brought from up to seventy miles away to feed the growing populations of the south-eastern valleys. These 'Cardi' carts were open, light vehicles, with a single upright rail at each side. They were usually painted a light red, and driven by the farmers or hired carriers. They came from Pembrokeshire, Carmarthenshire and Cardiganshire, piled high with vegetables, eggs, bacon and salted hams, as well as the carcasses of recently slaughtered pigs, feet in the air and decently covered with a white cloth. The carts travelled in groups of twelve for mutual protection, and they needed it. I have spoken with the grandson of one Cardiganshire farmer who was murdered for his money when he risked travelling alone on the Llandovery road. This whole round trip took the farmers about a week; they would leave early on Monday morning and return on Saturday. They were mostly trading in Merthyr Tydfil, when the new iron works had made that small Breconshire village into the largest industrial town in South Wales. In the eighteenth century, strings of mules also made their way into Merthyr from the Breconshire farms. They carried the produce in panniers which were filled with coal for the return journey.

Although we shall be making this journey in the reverse direction from the drovers and the drivers of the Cardi carts on their way to the markets, this east to west stretch will enable you to make a circular walk back to Cross Inn. So turn left at 160:874292 and follow the track of the old Roman road as it climbs uphill along the ridge of Mynydd Bach Trecastell. Just over a mile beyond the highest point on this ridge (160:846300) you can discover two more half-hidden stone circles if you climb up the hillside by the path to your right. Beside the circles are the enfolded earthworks of Y Pigwn. These carefully arranged terraces were once the formidable defences of a strategic line of communication from which the Romans hoped to control the movements of the rebellious Silures, the tenacious Celtic tribe which fought bitterly to retain its lands in south Wales. The banks mark interlocking enclosures, the smaller set at a slight diagonal inside the larger, the south-east corners of the two actually running across the road. Now only the semi-wild herds of horses graze the grassy mounds and negotiate the marshy land at either side of the old road.

Past the Roman camp, the Roman road deflects from its arrow-

Carreg Cennen castle in Dynevor.

Lane by Carreg Cennen.

straight course to keep to the high ground above a steep valley. If you follow that way, you will find that from this height you can look west to the mountains of Dyfed, a timely reminder of the territory that has been covered, now that we have come about halfway.

Once you have got round the valley, you will find that the track descends abruptly to a stream by a gate leading to a perpetually muddy, narrow lane serving Hafod Fawr (160:814313). On a map of 1905, 'Black Cock', possibly indicating an inn, is marked on the north side of the track as you leave the moor and come down to this gate, and the hilly, narrow road to Halfway on the A40.

This is all a diversion from the main course of the circular walk which continues south-west from Y Pigwn, by the track that keeps to the fairly dry ridgeway of a marshy hillside. If you go straight to it, you will notice on your right, as you leave the Roman road to follow this route, that you can just make out further earthworks, believed to have been a Roman signal station. When you come to a meeting place of tracks (160:815302), you could make another small digression by climbing up to the hill to the south-west to look at Tomen y Rhos, one of the major cairns in this area of pre-Celtic burial mounds and ritual monuments.

The final stage of the walk, however, lies to the south-east along the edge of the forest, and you reach that path by going downhill across the marshes. You will find drier paths further to your left as you leave the ridgeway track, if the ground is too wet. You would in any case be more authentic in taking them, for no drover would walk animals across wet

On the moor by Y Pigwn.

land, if it could be avoided. After a couple of miles, when this path has left the trees behind and gone past the old quarries from which roofing stone was taken in the nineteenth century, it makes a steep descent to the lane which runs south to Cross Inn. If you want to complete this walk by visiting Myddfai, you should turn right as soon as you get off the hill. The village is a couple of miles away to the north-west.

Riding stable
Mrs Lesley M.K. Gibbins
Blue Well Riding Centre Ffynnonlas
Llanllwni
Pencader
Dyfed SA399AY
The routes to the east of Brechfa and north of Gwernogle, mentioned on page 108 are bridleways; but unfortunately a locked gate and a stile will prevent you riding along the north bank of the Cothi to Edwinsford from Abergorlech.

The slopes of Carreg Cennen.

Chapter 6

Gower and Glamorgan

It was not only from the extreme south-west that the cattle converged on the Swansea markets and livestock fairs. They also came from the scattered coastal farms of the Gower peninsula, and so before following the herds on their long journey to the crossing of the Wye or the shorter land route to the Bristol Channel, I should like to look at the routes taken by the drovers bringing beasts to Swansea from the Gower and the surrounding country.

In 1905, the voluble Devon parson Sabine Baring-Gould pronounced that a week might well be spent in the exploration of Gower, declaring that it 'must be done on foot or bicycle, as there are no trains to carry the traveller from place to place'. Now that cars clog the lanes in summer and bicycling is at worst impossible and at best uncomfortable, his words have an almost cynical ring. Yet it is possible, on foot or horseback, to find areas of the peninsula that are comparatively isolated.

A I shall describe two such routes from the farms in the western parts of the Gower heading east towards Swansea. The first starts at Kingshall Farm (159:434893) two miles due west of Llanddewi. To get to Kingshall, take the path that climbs towards Rhossili Down from the B4247 by the farms at Pitton Cross (159:435879), and then turn north along the farm-track to Kingshall. This was once owned by the Lucases, members of an Essex family who came to the Gower in the Middle Ages and who grew to be one of the largest landowners on the peninsula. From their farmhouse on the western down, an old wide green lane runs east, straight to Llanddewi. On the way it passes Henllys, said to have been built by another powerful Gower family, the Mansells, who inherited the Penrice estate by marriage, and thereafter increased their holdings on the Gower through various profitable dynastic arrangements. They were not apparently totally against bending the law to suit their convenience, and are reputed to have used the spacious cellars behind Henllys

The coastline of Gower.

to conceal contraband goods brought by underground passage from the coast at Rhossili. It could well be so, for the Mansells of Henllys had a reputation for being very quick off the mark when a ship was driven on to these rocks.

The ancient settlement around the church of Llanddewi (St David's) has been the focus of surrounding farms since the Middle Ages. It was the Mansells who built the manor house across the road from the church in the sixteenth century, near the site of the former Bishop's Palace. Now Lake Farm just to the north of the church mainly serves as a caravan and camping park, but it also displays some of the farming methods and implements that were in use on the Gower at the end of the nineteenth century.

From Llanddewi you take the road east to Knelston, whence a path goes south-east across the fields, past traces of earthworks, to the small group of farms at Berry. South-east again from there, the road that serves those farms continues over the hill to the path that leads round the edge of a wood to join the track to Hangman's Cross. Here, where several old roads meet, at a place also known as Cold Comfort, a

A Kingshall Farm → Swansea road 3 miles

B Broughton Burrows → Penmaen 12 miles

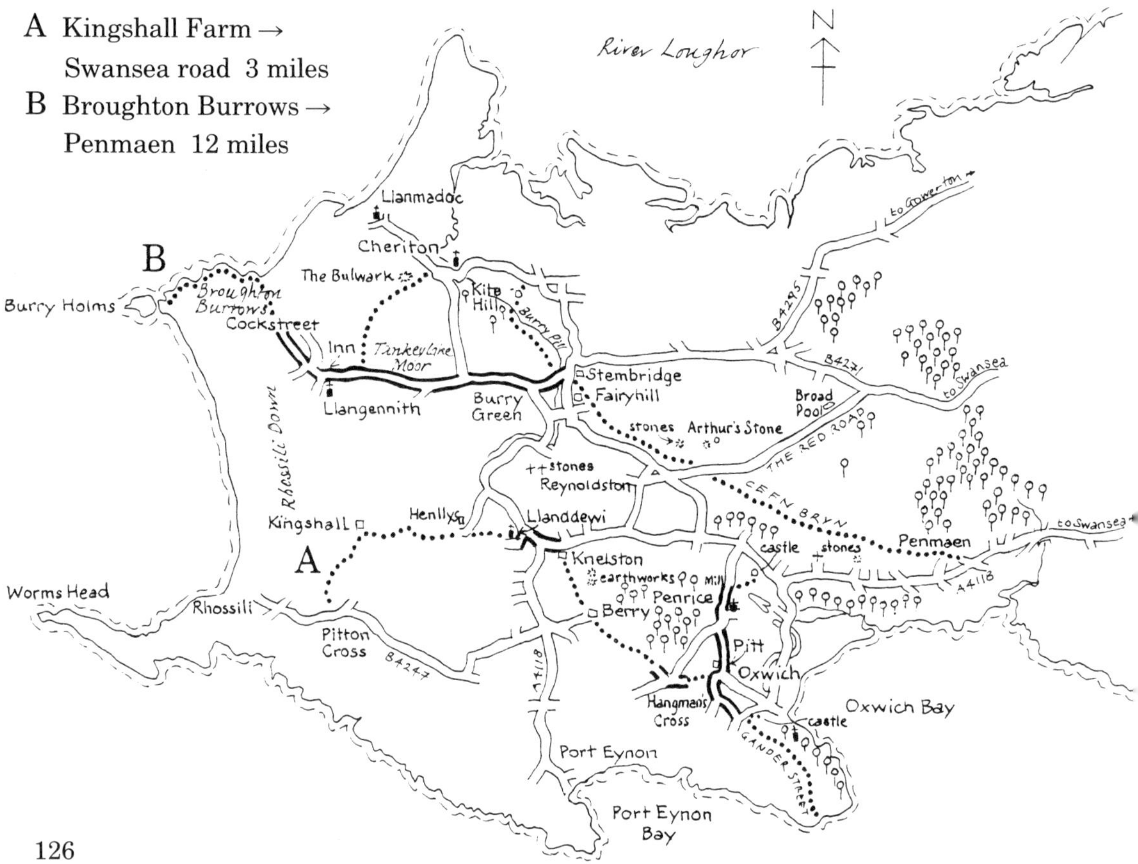

Old castle walls at Penrice.

wretched sheep stealer might meet up with the forces of law and the rights of property.

The bridlepath that goes downhill from here to the east is an old hollow-way, used until recently to take animals from one farm to another. It comes out on the lane just to the south of Pitt, an early seventeenth-century farmhouse, which originally belonged to the Bennetts, another long-standing Gower family. From here the lane goes north through Penrice village, and then makes a steep descent to the wooded valley beneath the grounds of Penrice castle and the Mansell mansion. Parallel to the present lane, you can trace the old track through the woods. It earned its name of Penny Hitch from the fee charged by a local farmer for the loan of a horse to help drag loads up the daunting slope.

To the left of the lane, when you reach the valley bottom, you will find that the old mill pond has been reconstructed in a clearing in the forest; and the ruins of the mill building are nearby. You will find leaflets about it here, and a series of waymarked walks through the woods; but your

Around Penrice castle.

Penrice woods.

way goes north through the castle grounds. Romantic and overgrown, rounded towers are all that remain of the castle that the Lords of Penrice built in the thirteenth century, and which was later inherited by the Mansells through marriage. To the north of it is the main high road to Swansea, now the A4118; and, to the south, the extensive, reed-covered marshes leading down to Oxwich Burrows and the sea.

If you want to take a look at that bit of coastline and the farms around Oxwich, take the lane from Pitt to Oxwich Green, and then follow the footpath above another castle, really a fortified manor house, built by Sir

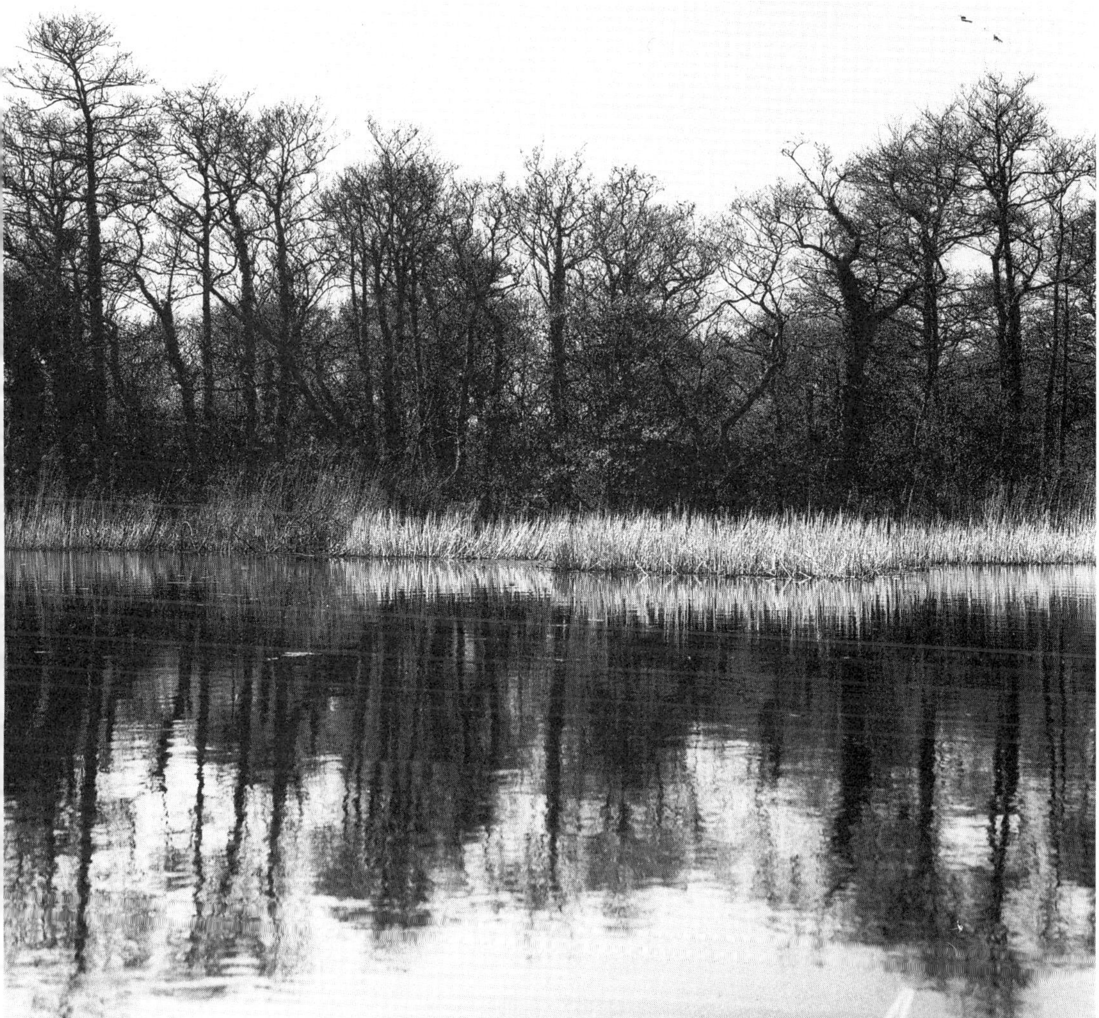

Oxwich marsh.

Rice Mansell, who had extended his fortune and powers at the Dissolution by acquiring Margam Abbey, and who wanted something more fitting than Penrice castle to match his rising status. The path above the castle goes to the limestone cliffs of Oxwich Point; however, if you go down to the bay past the castle, you will be walking along Gander Street, an indication to some antiquarians that this was a Roman road, but I suppose it could have been a goose street, and geese may have been shipped from the shingle below the church, where the pleasure yachts are moored now, and which serves as a gathering place for the holiday crowds. If you go back to the village from here, and then turn right, you will reach the main Swansea road, by the unfenced lane through the marshes, which are now a nature reserve.

B Because of the traffic, there is little point in going east of Penmaen along the A4118; this village will also be the goal of our second walk on the Gower which starts from the flower-laden sand dunes of Broughton Burrows on the north-west corner of the peninsula (159:416930). From here you go inland, south-east by the farm of Cockstreet to Llangennith, whose church, notable for its massive tower, crowned with a distinctive saddle-back roof, is the largest in the Gower.

Despite the caravan sites and all the impedimenta of the holiday industry, this village still retains much of the lively individuality that it must have possessed when it was a thriving weaving centre, and a collecting point for the cattle being driven to Reynoldston and Swansea. In those days, July 5th was the great day in Llangennith, the festival of Mapsant, when with great exuberance of drinking, prize-fighting and dancing, the young men proudly styling themselves 'Llangennith oxen' celebrated their founding saint, the gentle Cenydd. One tradition makes this saint the son of the British historian Gildas; another, more fanciful, claims that he was born in Brittany, the deformed offspring of incestuous union. The crippled babe was put in a basket of reeds and thrown into the sea, which was washed up on the northern shore of Gower. The full story is told in the church and includes a description of the 'titty' bell, from which the infant is said to have been nourished.

From the King's Head in Llangennith, the lane goes due east across Tankeylake Moor, a stretch of gorse-covered land between Llanmadoc Hill and Hardingsdown. This way will take you through Burry Green towards Stembridge and the beginning of the walk along Cefn Bryn, the diagonal ridgeway that links the north and south coasts of the peninsula. The path to the ridge starts just across a fork in the lane at 159:468915.

You can also reach that point by going over Llanmadoc Hill from Llangennith and making your way down its north-eastern slopes to Cheriton church by Burry Pill stream. On a clear day it is certainly worth climbing up through the gorse that covers this outcrop of red sandstone that broke through the surrounding limestone to form the hill, for although it only rises to 609 feet, you will find that it gives you a complete view of the western Gower. On the northern slopes of the hill, where the ponies mostly graze, you will come across Bronze Age cairns, and a formidable earthwork composed of interwoven banks and ditches. This enclosure, aptly named the Bulwark, served as a stockade for cattle when the Iron Age farmers found themselves under threat from hostile tribes, or even from the much more organized Roman invaders.

From the thirteenth-century church of St Cadog at Cheriton, a footpath goes along the banks of Burry Pill to the point where the stream is crossed by a track that comes south from Kite Hill. On the other side of the stream, the way goes over slightly higher ground to join the lane between Burry-green and Stembridge, and the start of the ridge route above Reynoldston.

You will begin this walk along a path to the east of Fairyhill, a gracious mansion built by the Lucases of Kingshall. Now a hotel, in the early nineteenth century it became the home of Lady Barham, a militant and energetic evangelist, who, like her more renowned friend, Hannah More, was determined to bring education and literacy to outlandish parts. If you looked at the chapel at Burry Green on the way here by the lane from Llangennith, you would have noticed an outer stairway leading to the gallery, where Lady Barham and her household had their high-backed pews.

The path from Fairyhill leads to a farm and the true beginning of the cairn-marked ridgeway that will bring you to Penmaen.

I have yet to find exact proof that the cattle and sheep from the farms in the north and west of the Gower were taken along this ridge on the way to the Swansea fairs, although in view of the marshy nature of the land on either side of it, I feel very confident that this was the way they were driven. Like all ridgeways, this four-mile spine of land has been a main line of communications for millennia. From its height you can look back to the Preseli Hills, and north and east to the Black Mountain, which we visited in the last chapter, and over to Pen y Fan and the Brecon Beacons which we shall come to in Chapter 8.

Only one road crosses the ridge, going to Reynoldston from the main road along the north side of the peninsula. It used to be known as the Red Road, before it was metalled, and was simply surfaced by the red sandstone that comprises the rock of the ridgeway. On one side of this road as it nears the ridge from the north is the site of a holy well, now enclosed as part of the public water system, and on the other (159:490900) a massive stone-covered neolithic burial chamber. Here again a prehistoric monument has been linked to King Arthur, for the flawed and massive capstone, believed to weigh 25 tons, is said to have been a pebble in the monarch's shoe.

You will find you are making a gradual climb as you go along the ridge south-east to Penmaen, before you descend into that village by Talbot's road, a part of the ancient route much used as a hunting road and carriage drive by the Mr Talbot who lived in the mansion by Penrice Castle during the nineteenth century.

A Scotch Pine Inn → Rhyd-y-fro 12 miles

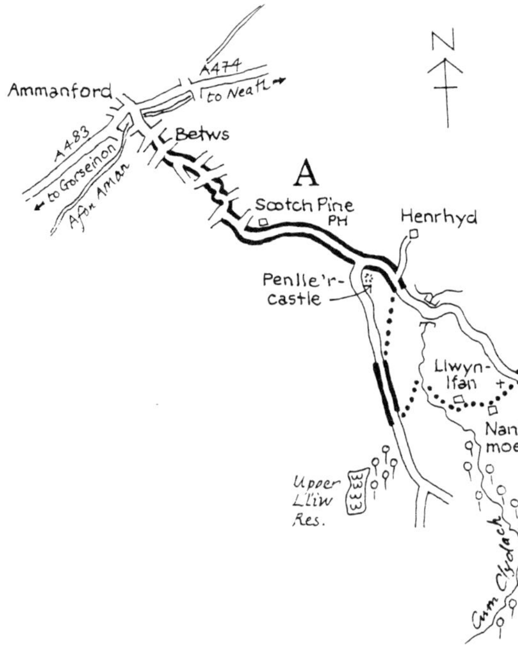

A Cattle fairs have been held in Swansea since the fifteenth century, and not all the beasts would have been brought there from the Gower. I now want to turn to look again at the country lying south-east of Carmarthen; starting across the Loughor river where the cattle were gathered at Betws (159: 633118), across the Amman from Ammanford, a town that did not exist until the coal mining started. From Betws the lane to the south-east, steep, narrow, winding and still much used by heavy lorries, climbs up to the Scotch Pine Inn. The name of this rather drab, low-lying pub indicates that it was once a stopping place for the drovers, where they could get some refreshment after the arduous haul to the high moors, and where the cattle might graze and gather strength for the journey across the wild and often marshy moorland to the east.

You can follow their route by taking the unfenced road from here to

Penlle'r Castle (159:665097). The oval ditch and earthwork that you will clamber on here surround a lost medieval village, whose dwellings are still roughly indicated by fragments of stone walls and mounds of turf. From this height, you can look south over Swansea and see the whole of the Gower stretching into the sea. When you come back to the moor you can either go along the lane running almost directly due south, or take the route followed by the cattle from the farm at Henrhyd (159:674101) across the steep valley to the north. That way starts from the lane running east behind the earthworks and joins the southerly lane as it goes down towards the Upper Lliw Reservoir.

Just before that lane reaches the forest on the east bank of the reservoir, you will find a path (159:669072) going to the north-east and then descending steeply to the valley of the Lower Clydach. On the hill above the eastern bank of the river you will pass the farm of Llwyn-Ifan, and, after crossing a second valley, come to Nant-moel and the farm road to a lane by a large, isolated church. This lane goes over Mynydd Carnllechart and then descends to the Upper Clydach river at the village of Rhyd-y-fro (160:713057) on the A474, six miles north of Neath.

Regular cattle fairs were held at Neath, which alternated with Cowbridge as the venue for the main south Wales agricultural show during the nineteenth century. From Neath the cattle were either driven directly east to be shipped from Porthcawl, if they were not to be taken along the coastal route to Cowbridge; or they went north-east towards Brecon.

Much of those latter routes will be described in Chapter 8, but I will look now at the way they start from the Neath valley; and, as the main mountain road between Neath and Brecon was subject to toll charges, I shall suggest that there is a good case to be made for the wilder and more isolated routes over the mountains to the north-east.

B The first follows the track marked as the Sarn Helen on the Ordnance Survey sheets. There is no doubt that this was a Roman road, linking Neath and Brecon; although not necessarily one planned by the redoutable Helen, Welsh wife of the Romano-British emperor Magnus Maximus. We shall follow it as far as a Roman auxillary camp south of Coelbren. To reach this section of the Sarn Helen, you must take the path through a belt of trees by leaving the A465 at 170:784003, just to the north-east of Aberdulais. This path climbs steeply past Llettybella Farm and comes out onto the open mountain side, and then turns right to run in a straight line north-east through a great forest.

The road is deflected by the rocks of Craig Clwyd Fechan (160:825061), turning to the west and going round the edge of the forest

B Neath → Roman camp 11 miles
C Tonna → Cefn Ffordd 7 miles

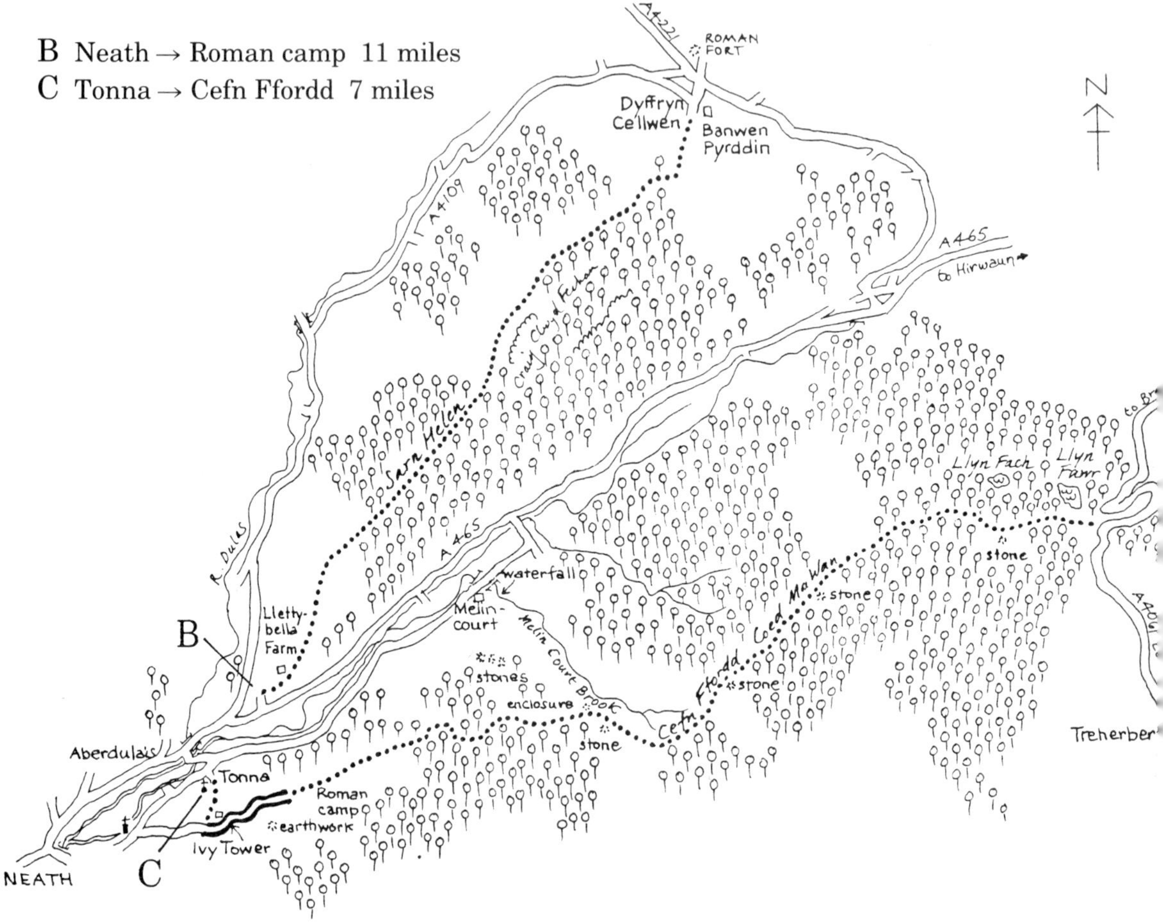

to rejoin its original course at 160:853084. From here it heads straight for the site of the Roman camp at 160:859109 to the north of Dyffryn Cellwen. On its way there it becomes for a short space the main street through the village of Banwen before crossing directly over the A4109.

This camp, partially excavated in 1904, was occupied until the middle of the second century. From it, the Sarn Helen runs towards the larger camp of Gaer just to the west of Brecon, and we shall follow it there during the course of the walks in Chapter 8.

C The other northern route from Neath starts at Tonna, across the river from Aberdulais, where the Neath Canal, built in the 1790s, joins the River Neath. Canal enthusiasts can well spend some time here looking

Melincourt waterfall.

at the lock basin, and the lock-keeper's house and stables, as well as the smithy and wood-seasoning shed and saw-pit, before resuming the route towards Brecon. You will do this by going south from Tonna church and then turning east towards the remains of another Roman camp at 170:796988. Here the old track goes through the forest for about three

Chapel at Melincourt.

miles, enters the valley of the Melin Court Brook and then climbs the precipitous ridge to Cefn Ffordd. The brook itself flows north-west to join the Neath, but not before dropping 80 feet to produce one of the most enchanting, enclosed falls (170:825018) in this valley of waterfalls, painted by Turner in 1795.

At Cefn Ffordd you are on the Coed Morgannwg Way, one of the most strenuous long-distance pathways through the mountains at the head of

Sheep in the
Rhondda valley.

Miners' town in the
Rhondda.

the south Wales valleys. It runs for 27 miles from Margam Country Park near Bridgend to the A4061 above Llyn Fawr, four miles north of Treherbert, a route that has always been heavily forested.

We leave it here, at the head of the Rhondda valley, for the route to the north has been disturbed by active open-cast mining, and that is another story. However, in Chapter 8, I will return to this route from Neath and trace its course north-east to Merthyr Tydfil and Brecon.

D John Fox, who wrote the *General View of the Agriculture of the County of Glamorgan* for the Board of Agriculture in 1796, described the channel road running east from Neath as 'beautiful and picturesque'. He was even so enchanted with 'the swelling sails of commerce' that the infant iron works and coal mines in no way detracted from the religious fervour with which he viewed 'the sublimity of nature' as he traversed the countryside and was inspired by it to 'a grateful adoration of Divine Power, Wisdom and Goodness'. He was fortunate in his creature comforts too, relishing the hostelries he visited and particularly the inn at Pyle (170:826824), which he found to be 'a distinguished instance of the exercise of private munificence for the convenience of the public'.

Some of the views he enjoyed still remain, although commerce, in the shape of the now tenuous steel works at Port Talbot, has immensely altered the countryside he knew; while 'the exercise of private munificence for the convenience of the public' has resulted in an enormous caravan park by the Ogmore estuary.

I start the next walk from the Porthcawl suburb of Newton (170:837775) because we know that there was a toll gate at Fox's Pyle Inn and another in the village itself along the mail road to Port Talbot. We also know that the Cowbridge Trust, which ran from Laleston (170:875799) to the Roman road which starts at Brocastle halfway between the Ewenny river and Cowbridge, had fourteen gates in the space of six miles. As it makes sense for us to follow a route to the south of that road, I have decided to begin by following the path round the northern edge of the sand-dunes that make up Merthyr Mawr Warren. This will take us past the remains of Candleston Castle, a fifteenth-century fortified manor house, whose lands lie beneath the encroaching sands, where the Lord of the Manor once bred his money-spinning rabbits.

From the car park by the castle ruins, it is worthwhile following the lane round to the church of Merthy Mawr (170:883775), which dates from the middle of the nineteenth century and has an elegant charm, unusual for its period. It was built for the planned estate village of thatched cottages, set up by Sir John Nicholl, a diehard reactionary, who

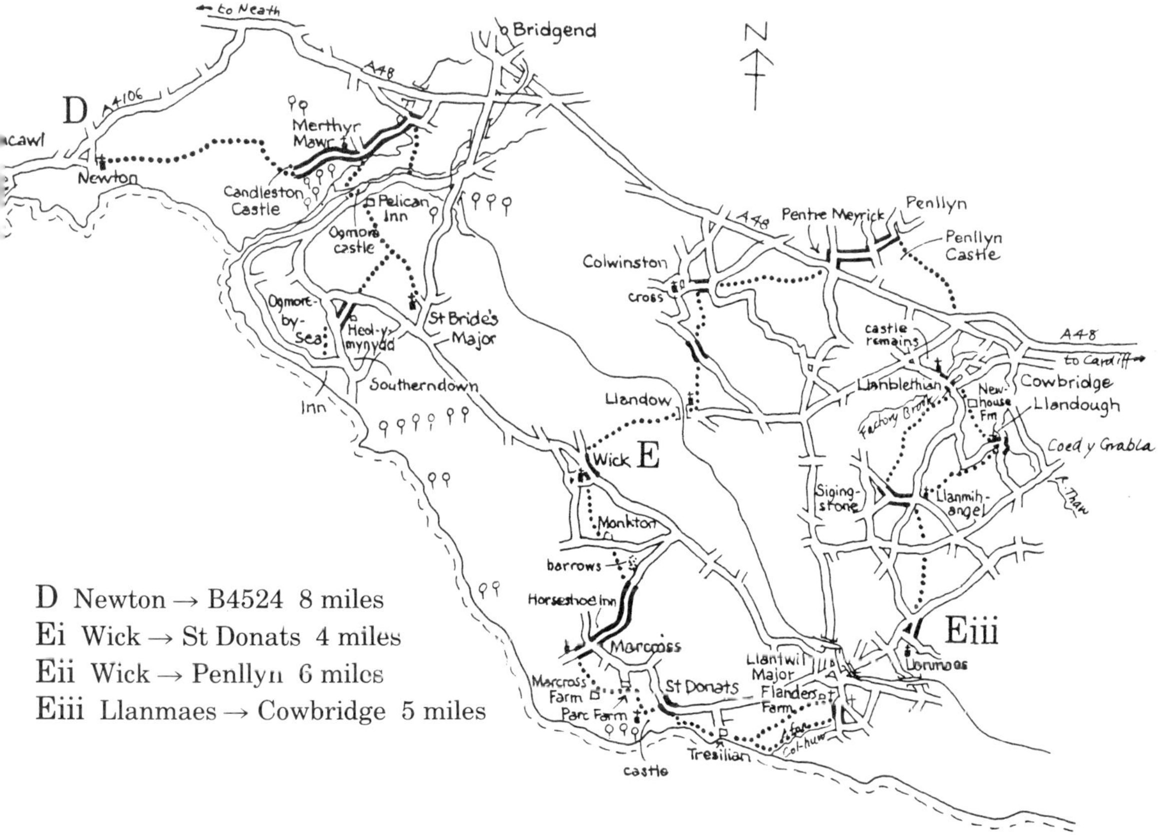

made his parkland in the area upstream by the Ogmore River having built his mansion there in the early years of the century.

From that landowner we will now go back in time to the twelfth-century ruin of the keep of Ogmore castle (170:882768). The lane going south from Merthyr Mawr church leads to a stretch of open pasture then to a little bridge over the Ogmore River and stepping stones set across the Ewenny River which flows by the ancient walls, where sheep graze beneath broken battlements.

There are many tales about these stepping stones, brought to this place from a ford near the church. Their origin probably led to their pious title of the steps of St Teilo. According to one secular tale they were put across the river by a lady of the castle, so that her lover could visit her from the further bank. In later years they were used for quite a different purpose, as the Baptist ministers waded out into the river beside the stones from which the candidates were lowered to be immersed in the water.

Dovecote at Llantwit Major.

The cattle heading east did not negotiate the stepping stones, they would either have been driven across the Ogmore through the ford at Merthyr or over the medieval bridge to the north of the park. Here a footpath goes between the two rivers to a crossing of the Ewenny where Verville Farm stands on the north bank and Tymaen on the south.

From the Pelican, the pub above the Ewenny on the same side as Ogmore castle, you can climb up past the golf course over Ogmore Down, turning south-west to Heol-y-mynydd (170:882751). From here you can either carry on towards the coast by taking the lane south to Groes Farm, where a footpath goes downhill across the moor to the B4524

Stepping stones by Ogmore castle.

between Ogmore and Southerndown and the road to St Bride's Major; or you can carry on east across the downs to the church of that village.

From there you can set out to explore the routes along which the droves converged on the market towns of Llantwit Major and Cowbridge. The latter has a long history as the capital of the Vale of Glamorgan. It stands on the course of the A48, a route that was known to the Romans; the medieval town, whose south gate still survives, could trace its history back to the Normans. Cowbridge was granted its first charter in 1254, and from that date its fairs and markets were meeting places for farmers and herdsmen for miles around. Yet, despite the town's importance, it would still have seemed a small village to us, as indeed it did to Francis Gose, author of *The Antiquities of England and Wales*. He came here in 1775 and found 'a single street of houses, some good but the major part only thatched cottages not unlike an Irish town'. At fair time this single street (now a wide and busy thoroughfare) was thronged with cattle and sheep who would be driven east from here towards Cardiff and Newport until the railway began to take over from the drovers in the 1860s.

We will follow that route through to the east in the next chapter. Now I want to explore the part of Glamorgan that lies between the Ewenny to the west and the Thaw, which flows to the sea through Flemingston Moor, in the east.

Ei I will begin by looking at a coastal route through St Donats (170:935683) to Llantwit Major. From St Bride's Major the B4265 runs south-east to Wick and we shall leave it there by the footpath that starts off beside the school (170:924720) and goes south to Monkton. Cross the lane here, and follow a continuation of the original path past a group of barrows. It will bring you to a lane going south to the Horseshoe Inn by the crossroads at Marcross. Carry straight on to the church, where you will find the path going south-east from here along the hill above the cliffs to Marcross Farm. Carry on east to the Parc Farm, and then turn south through the densely wooded valley that encloses the church of St Donats.

You will find the local centenarians listed in the church porch. They include a Francis Styck, who was 108 when he died in 1671. The drovers on their way to the fair at Llantwit Major would have been a familiar sight to him, and he would also have known the parsonage and cottages that are now ivy-covered ruins among the undergrowth of the surrounding wood: a settlement destroyed as recently as 1901, when Morgan Williams, a colliery owner from Aberpergwm, bought St Donats castle. He bought it from a descendant of the Stradlings who had lived there

(*Right*) The Bristol Channel at Nash Point.

St Donats church.

since 1257, and whose elaborate monuments Francis Styck would have seen in the church. He would also have been familiar with the stone calvary in the churchyard. Set up and carved in the fifteenth century, it is a rare survival of the desecrations of the Reformation.

The path going up the valley from the church takes you past the castle, now serving as an international sixth form, and widely know as Atlantic College. It was endowed by the American newspaper magnate William Randolph Hearst, who bought the castle in 1925.

(*Right*) Atlantic College, St Donats.

When you come to the lane at the castle gates turn right and very soon you will find you can make your way along a path, by turning right again. This will lead you to a cliff-top walk past Tresilian House. From here you can either turn inland to walk through the fields towards Flanders Farm, or continue along the cliff until you reach the steps that go down to the beach and the path that goes into the town along the west bank of the Afon Col-huw. If you take the first route you will find yourself beside the much beloved double church of St Illtud, from whom the town of Llantwit Major derives its Welsh name of Llanilltud Fawr. The eastern and most recent part of this building was attached as an addition to the old collegiate church in the west of the little valley, and here you will find many memorials of the Celtic church and the college in which Illtud trained his missionary saints, who set out across the channel from here through England's south-west peninsula to Brittany. As you walk, however, you will be more immediately fascinated by the corbelled dovecote, a medieval building set up when the Abbot of Tewkesbury held these lands.

Eii The next walk in this area goes north-west from Wick (170:924724) across the fields to Llandow, which you reach by crossing Sutton Brook and going under the railway to the Alun river. Just past the church, follow another path going north to Stembridge Brook. You will cross the brook as you turn left along the lane (170: 944743), and then you will take the field-path on your right to Colwinston. Turn right again when you come to that village, and then go straight ahead at the old crossroads (where the lane forms a T junction). You are now on a farm road to Pentre Meyrick on the A48, just over a mile to the west of Cowbridge. You can avoid returning to Cowbridge on the main road by taking the lanes north through Penllyn (170:975765) and then walking along the path that goes south-east through the woods which surround Penllyn Castle. This is an eighteenth-century mansion built onto a solitary, surviving medieval tower. This path will bring you out on the road that by-passes the centre of Cowbridge to the north.

Eiii Our last walk in this area starts from Llanmaes to the north of Llantwit Major, and comes into Cowbridge through its ancient southern gate or through the substantial suburb of Llanblethian. We will now be walking in an area familiar to Cowbridge's best known citizen, the eccentric Edward Williams, who chose the pseudonym Iola Morganwg. He was born in 1746 near Flemingston, the son of a stonemason. He was only nine years old when he started to learn his father's trade, and as a young man he went to London to dress the stones for the new Blackfriars Bridge.

There he fell into political and literary company, becoming a friend of

Benjamin Franklin, Tom Paine and Pitt; while Cowper and Boswell were among those who hailed him as the Welsh Bard. Yet he still longed for home, and at the age of thirty-one came back to Glamorgan. Southey, who himself contemplated a move to the Vale of Neath, was later to pen verses for the polymath Welshman he had known in London:

> Iola, old Iola, he who knows
> The virtues of all herbs of mount or vale,
> Or greenwood shade, or quiet brooklet's bed;
> Whatever lore of science or of song
> Sages and bards of old have handed down.

Eventually Edward Williams opened a shop, selling books, stationery and groceries on a site near the present town hall in Cowbridge. Here he was able to express his strong opposition to the slave trade by announcing that the sugar he sold came from the East Indies, and so was 'the only sugar uncontaminated with human blood'.

Two circumstances seem to have started a misplaced belief that he was a notable drover. The first probably stems from the fact that he had a wide knowledge of local farming conditions, and, as a close friend of Walter Davies, helped in the preparation of the *General View of the Agriculture of South Wales* for the newly formed Board of Agriculture. The second arises from his propensity for long-distance walking, which was also linked to his strong political beliefs. He happened to be in Bristol when the church bells rang out in joy at the defeat of Wilberforce's anti-slavery bill, and he was so disgusted that he shook the dust of the city from his shoes, made for the Severn estuary, crossed to Black Rock and walked home without stopping. No drover would have subjected himself or his animals to such an ordeal; nor would any of them have been so absorbed in their books as he was while employed to look after the parsonage animals. When the owner came back he found pigs, geese, ducks and fowls disporting themselves all over the house.

Although Iola was no drover he was certainly a familiar sight along the lanes and highways of Glamorgan until his death in 1826. This extraordinary little man stalked along, alternately stretching up to hold his walking stick high in the air in order to hold his asthma at bay by exercising his chest, and bending low over a book. For he nearly always read as he walked, a pencil in his stick-free hand in order to mark significant passages. At the age of seventy-three he tramped to Carmarthen, refusing to ride the horse that his son had given him; but as he delighted in the animal's company, he had it walking behind him like a dog, and cheerfully paid the tolls that it engendered on the turnpike roads.

Our own more modest walk from Llanmaes goes across the fields to the saddle-back tower of Llanmihangel on the further side of the narrow valley. There are two routes to explore from here. The first goes east and starts from the path behind the church, climbing uphill to the woods that run to the banks of the Thaw. Before you reach the river, turn left along a path that leaves the wood, crosses a stream and climbs up to Llandough. Here we are once more in the domain of the Mansells, whom we met on the Gower. For two hundred years from 1677, this powerful family owned the hill-top castle here, and had rights over the manor lands. A footpath goes north-west from that castle to Newhouse Farm (170:991735) and the lane to Llanblethian. Here you will come across the impressive gateway leading to the ruins of another castle, built to defend this highway through mid-Glamorgan.

The second route from Llanmihangel goes west along the lane towards Sigingstone. Before you get to that village, take the lane on your right (170:977718), then turn right again along a field-path which will bring you into Llanblethian to the west of Newhouse Farm. This time you will come into the village (now a suburb of Cowbridge) by the road that climbs steeply to the medieval hill-top church.

As you come into the wide main street of Cowbridge, it is fairly easy, despite the heavy traffic and the modern shops, to imagine how it would have been when hundreds of cattle and sheep were brought to be sold here. The main market area until the middle of the nineteenth century was at the junction of High Street and Church Street. The town hall and the town cross were here, both being removed in 1830, when the new town hall was set up near the site of Iola Morganwg's shop. Not surprisingly, at that time and for most of the preceding century, the main occupation of wealthy Cowbridge citizens was retailing and inn-keeping. The more splendid of the hostelries catered for travellers along the main route linking Cardiff to west Wales; but there was also provision for the farmers and drovers, who completed their deals here, and then headed east with the herds.

Chapter 7

From Cardiff to the Wye

Along the coast of the Bristol Channel from Cardiff to Caldicot open marshland, much like the Somerset moors across the water, divides the uplands from the sea. During the eighteenth and nineteenth centuries large numbers of calves were reared here, the pastures being let to the farmers who lived on the higher ground to the north. The animals so reared proved to be thirty to forty per cent larger than the stock that never left the upland farms; but in November, when the land, much of which lies below sea level, became 'wet and poachy', they had to be taken off the marshes. If they were left there during the winter months they were liable to a disease that could well deprive them of the use of their hind legs.

Early in the summer, a good many of the cattle that had grazed the levels the previous year were sold to the drovers for the English markets; some of them were shipped to Somerset from the old port of Sully (171:152679), described by Leyland as 'a praty havenet of socour for shippes'. Many of these animals would then be taken to Bridgwater for re-sale at the Somerset fairs discussed in the Introduction.

The overland route to the English markets went along roads considered by Charles Hassall (who also wrote in the 1790s on the state of agriculture in Glamorgan) to be models of good road making. These roads have now become the A48 and the M4; so, instead of following the drovers directly from Cardiff and Newport through Magor (171:425873), I suggest that we explore the sea coast and the levels between Newport and Caldicot, although if you have time it is also good to walk along the lanes and droves of the Wentlooge levels to the west.

Magor church stands to the south of a pleasing little square in the centre of a village, which has managed to keep its distinctive character despite having been subsumed into a suburb of Newport. The large porch is the most impressive part of this church building; but if you look to the west of the churchyard, you will find the surprising ruins of a

Newport power station from St Bride's on the Wentlooge levels.

substantial fourteenth-century mansion. This was once the dwelling of the local Procurator, a priest whose unpopular duty it was to collect dues to send to Rome. To compensate him for the dislike of his fellows, he was enabled to live in flagrant opulence; and these ruins of his impressive house form a rare medieval monument. Back in the square, followers of the cattle trade will be intrigued by an unusual war memorial, commemorating David Alfred Thomas, who died in 1918, 'serving the nation as a food controller'.

A Beside the church, the lane going south crosses over the railway, and if you then turn left, you can see through the fence across the road, aligned to the east end of the church, traces of the ancient causeway across Whitewall Common leading south to Lower Grange Farm, once the property of Tintern Abbey. That old route runs through an important nature reserve, and the official public right of way has been diverted along the lane that goes east of the common to Magor Pill Farm (171:434858).

The more interesting route runs through part of this rich marshland reserve, managed by the Gwent Wildlife Trust (16 White Swan Court, Monmouth NP5 3NY). As you can enter only with their permission, you should get in touch with the trust or the warden, Derek Upton (0291 420137) if you want to explore the area more extensively. For the purpose of this walk however, you can cross the reserve by a public footpath if you turn west after you have crossed the railway line from Magor, and then take the unsigned, open drove on your left.

Magor means 'the place of the walls', and it is along this drove, locally known as Blackwall, that you can actually see heavy squares of worked limestone beneath the undergrowth above the draining ditch or 'reen', as these cuttings are called in south Wales and Somerset. These stones are the remains of one of the Roman walls heading inland from the sea. Soon you will cross the traces of Rush Wall, another piece of Roman engineering running from west to east. Just before you reach it, you will find a path on your left which will take you through the marshes and water meadows of the reserve. Here great poplars grow along the banks of the reens, and among the grasses you will find colonies of ragged robin, the unusual spineless meadow thistle and pervasive yellow rattle. This path goes by a swamp of Norfolk reed, used for thatching dwellings along the estuary from prehistoric times.

This way goes east, and brings you across the meadows to the lane leading from Magor to Magor Pill Farm. Here, at the official entrance to the reserve, is the hut that houses a display of the natural and human history of these levels. Now as you follow the lane to the south, you will probably notice that the high raked centre of the macadam is cracking — a deterioration caused by yet another Roman wall, whose ancient stones keep erupting through the works of present-day road builders.

If you are going directly along the coastal levels to Caldicot, then you

A Magor → Goldcliff 9 miles
B Magor → Portskewett 9 miles

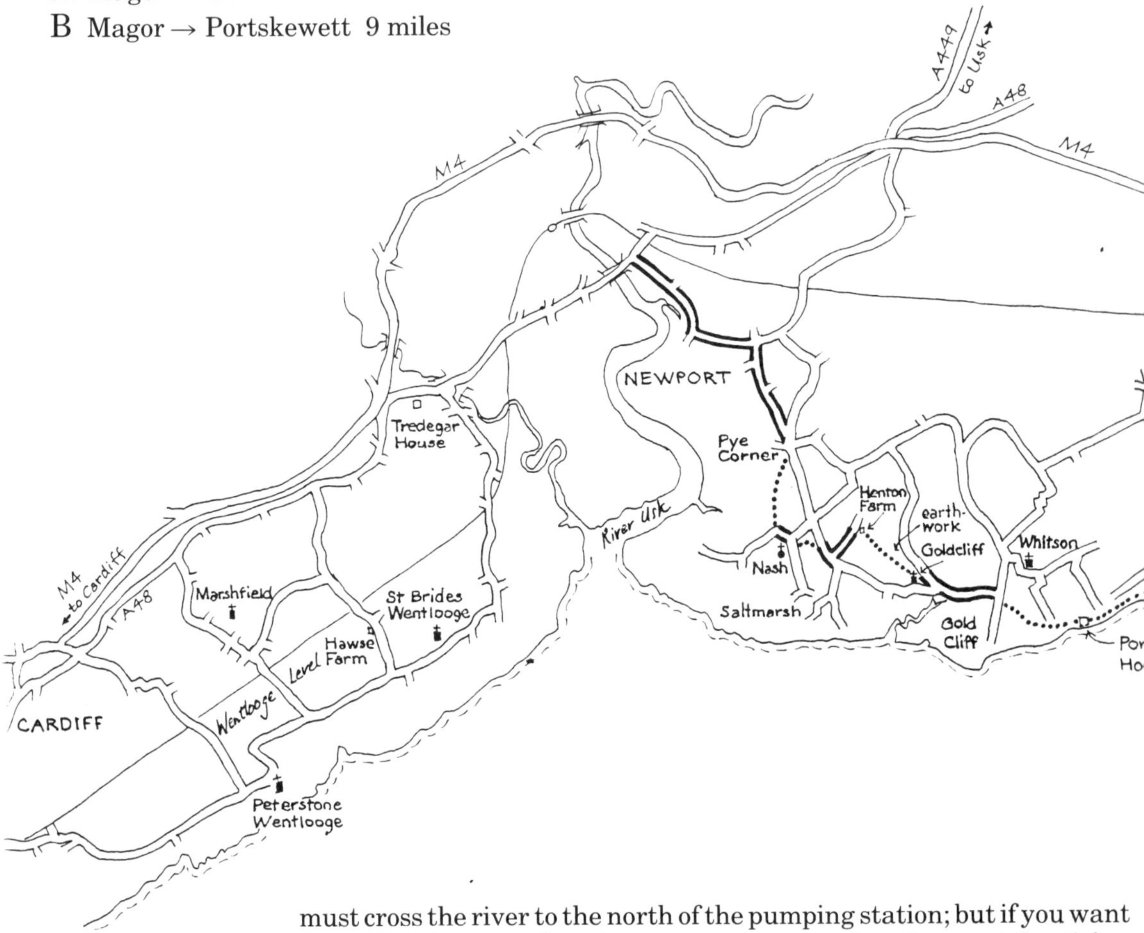

must cross the river to the north of the pumping station; but if you want to explore the sea wall to the west, carry on south to the coastal path by the sea wall. Walk along it for a couple of miles westwards to Porton House, above the submerged forest lying beneath the waters of the Bristol Channel, traces of which are visible at low tide. This area was once a base for smugglers, and a salmon painted on the wall of one of the cottages is a reminder that salmon have been fished here ever since the Romans started reclaiming the land from the sea in the third century, and probably even before that. A Roman fish basket has been found here, and it is thought that in medieval times these salmon fisheries supplied the money that ensured the English victory at Agincourt.

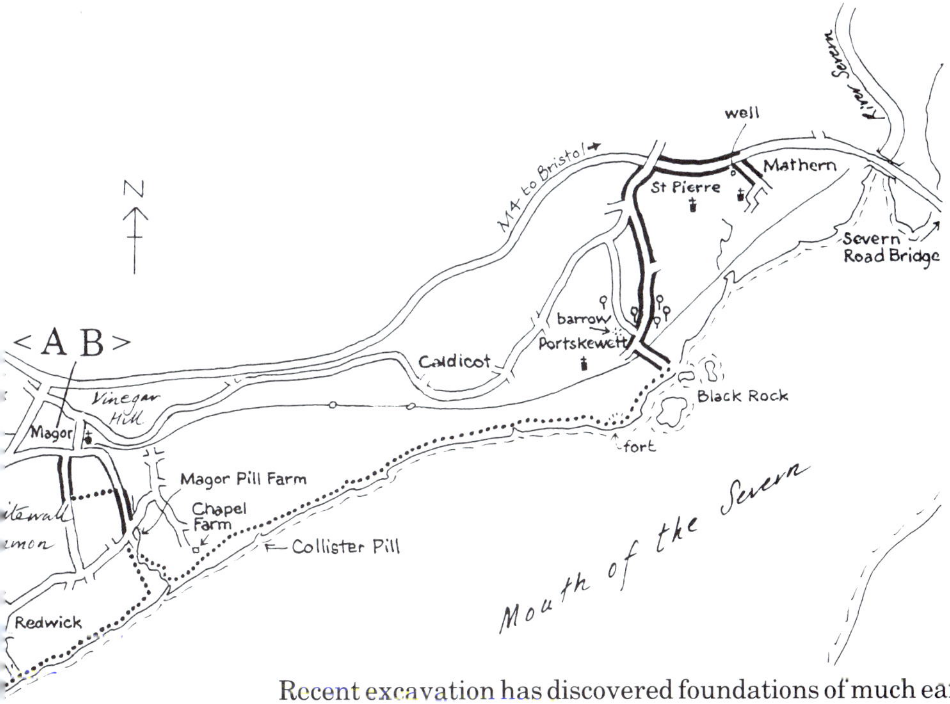

Recent excavation has discovered foundations of much earlier Iron Age settlements by Goldcliff, where there are even some traces of mesolithic inhabitants.

From Porton House, you must go inland on the footpath going north-west, crossing some of the drainage reens in order to reach the lane for Goldcliff village. Gold Cliff itself, a slight eminence above the channel, once really lived up to its name, but now the glistening rock is covered in the great limestone blocks of the sea wall.

The slightly raised ground that forms the 'cliff' is now topped by a modern hexagonal building at the edge of a farm, reached by a wide-verged lane, the few houses being set well back from the road. This route once served both as a sheep-drove and place where the animals were penned while awaiting transportation across the channel.

If you can face the slippery mud, walking carefully in order to put your feet on the harder ridges of blue clay, an exploration of the inter-tidal stretch to the west of Goldcliff will take you back initially to the mesolithic and then through to the comparatively recent Iron Age; for the posts, wattle walling and reed flooring of two huts dating from around 300 BC have recently been discovered here, together with a network of raised trackways used by the inhabitants to cross the marsh that has now formed into peat. The posts that mark these constructions have been preserved by the high tides that cover them twice a day.

Wetlands chapel.

Farm building on Caldicot moor.

Clearly the Severn Sea has widened considerably over the centuries, and the mud of the sea bed, that you are sliding about on, was once top soil that produced pasture for wild auroch, whose bones have been discovered here. Dung from more recent animals has been found by the Iron Age huts, indicating that the people who lived in them were farmers as well as fishermen; and from the clue of a wolf's tooth, archaeologists judge that their predecessors in this place were among the first people to domesticate a canine companion and work force.

From the western Gold Cliff foreshore you can walk to the Farmer's Boy pub in Goldcliff village back across the marshes and water meadows. Along this foreshore you will find the gloriously edible samphire (why did Shakespeare think it was a plant of fearsome cliffs?); the tall

On Caldicot moor.

seed-spikes of henbane; sea spurry; marsh mallow; and slender hare's ear.

To the north-east you will see the leaning tower of Whitson, and if you visit the church there, you will find an inscription five feet above the ground recording the depth of the flood level in January 1607. It gives force to the local name of the slightly higher land to the east of Magor Pill. The wide causeways in that area are known as Noah's Ark because they provided refuges for the animals in times of flood. That was a common hazard, and during that early seventeenth-century flood, destruction was so severe that, according to a contemporary account quoted by Sabine Baring-Gould, 'All kinds of cattle being for twenty-foure miles in length and fowre in breadth, were dronded.'

B If you are heading towards Newport from Goldcliff, you will take the path from the church along the side of the drainage reen to Henton Farm and then take the footpaths to Nash and on to Pye Corner on the outskirts of the city.

However, our main route from Magor Pill runs to the east of Magor along part of the sea wall, a twenty-mile stretch of grassy bank shored up with stone, extending from the mouth of the Rhymney almost as far as Chepstow. It was once thought to have been built by the Romans; but, the engraved stone excavated at Gold Cliff in 1875 that gave rise to such a speculation is now thought to commemorate a drainage scheme, of which the walls running inland to Magor may have formed a part.

To make this journey east along the coast, you must start, as we have seen, by crossing the river by the field-paths running inland behind the pumping station at Magor Pill. For a mile or so the way goes along the sea wall, above the wide inter-tidal marshes to Collister Pill. Out in the channel you will see the rock of Denny Island, jokingly referred to as Undy Village Green, once that actual common space had been concreted over to form the inevitable car park in the village to the east of Magor. Behind the rock on the Avon side of the water are the twin, industrial towers of Portishead, a world away from these lonely marshes, where the banks of the drainage channels are splendid with bursts of yellow flag, and linnets swoop in their graceful idiosyncratic flights above the mud flats. Even the World War II gun emplacement by Chapel Farm does not seem too incongruous, for, instead of the usual concrete structure, it is surprisingly built of patterned bricks.

A mile or so to the east of Collister Pill you will find that you are entering a Ministry of Defence area, where it can be dangerous to walk. So if the red flag flies you will have to go inland and walk along the causeway to the south of Caldicot Moor.

Ruins of the Procurator's house at Magor.

Caldicot castle.

If you make a detour and take this opportunity to visit Caldicot's castle and the recently discovered Bronze Age boat, you will find that you can look north, past the Roman town in the plain at Caerwent to the hills of Wentwood Forest which lie between the coast and the larger Roman garrison at Usk. We will look at those places in the next walk; now our way lies to the east along the coastal path south of Portskewett, through Sudbrook, where the train emerges from the Severn tunnel.

The old ferry passage across the estuary, operating until the railway tunnel was built, went from Black Rock (162:515881), and you will find that, having crossed the railway track, you can make your way down to the water there. In the early years of the nineteenth century the passen-

(*Right*)
The Severn Bridge.

ger boats to the English shore took about fifty minutes to make the crossing, and cattle, sheep and pigs on their way to Bristol and the south-east would have been taken over in much the same time. On August 17th, 1763, Wesley made the crossing in the opposite (westerly) direction, taking the boat which had just brought a herd of oxen from Wales into England.

The lane going north from here towards Porskewett and the B4245 was the toll road that linked Chepstow with the ferry. Follow it until you see the sign to St Pierre Farm on your right. It leads to a large hotel surrounded by an enormously affluent-looking golf course. Do not be intimidated. You are perfectly entitled to walk through the hotel courtyard and it is certainly worth doing so for the sake of the magnificent three-storey, sixteenth-century gateway and the Norman church, where the Crown Jewels were held as security against a loan made by the Lord of the Manor to enable Henry V to conduct his French wars.

From this church, it is unfortunately no longer possible to take the footpath east to Mathern; now if you would visit that ancient church where the fifth century Tewdric is buried you must get there along the roads. For three hundred years from the early fifteenth century, the Bishop of Llandaff had his palace here. The remains of that building are in private hands, but you can climb the tall tower of the church beside it and look back over much of the territory we have traversed.

The walk finishes here, for although you can make your way by lane and footpath to the A466 linking Chepstow to the M4, that is really no road for a pedestrian to enjoy. We will see how the cattle went north to cross the Wye in the last walk in this section; but before doing that I want to trace the links between Magor and Usk.

C Leave Magor by the lane that goes under the motorway and runs north-east, then leave it (171:424886) for the parallel footpath to the west, running along the hillside of a wooded valley to rejoin the lane by the church that served the lost village of St Bride's Netherwent. Continue north from here until you find a footpath climbing up to Penhow Castle and its church, set on a steep and rocky knoll. The much renewed church has a tower dating from 1913 and a few twelfth-century remains. The castle, which you can visit from Easter to the end of September, is also a mixture of ages, having some medieval walls attached to a three-storey eighteenth-century house.

North of the castle a path leads down to the A48 to the west of the Castle Arms Inn. This hostelry served travellers on the London to Cardiff road from the sixteenth century until it was closed down in 1868. Until 1742, it was known as the Rock, sharing its name with the farm,

In Wentwood forest.

C Magor → Usk 14 miles

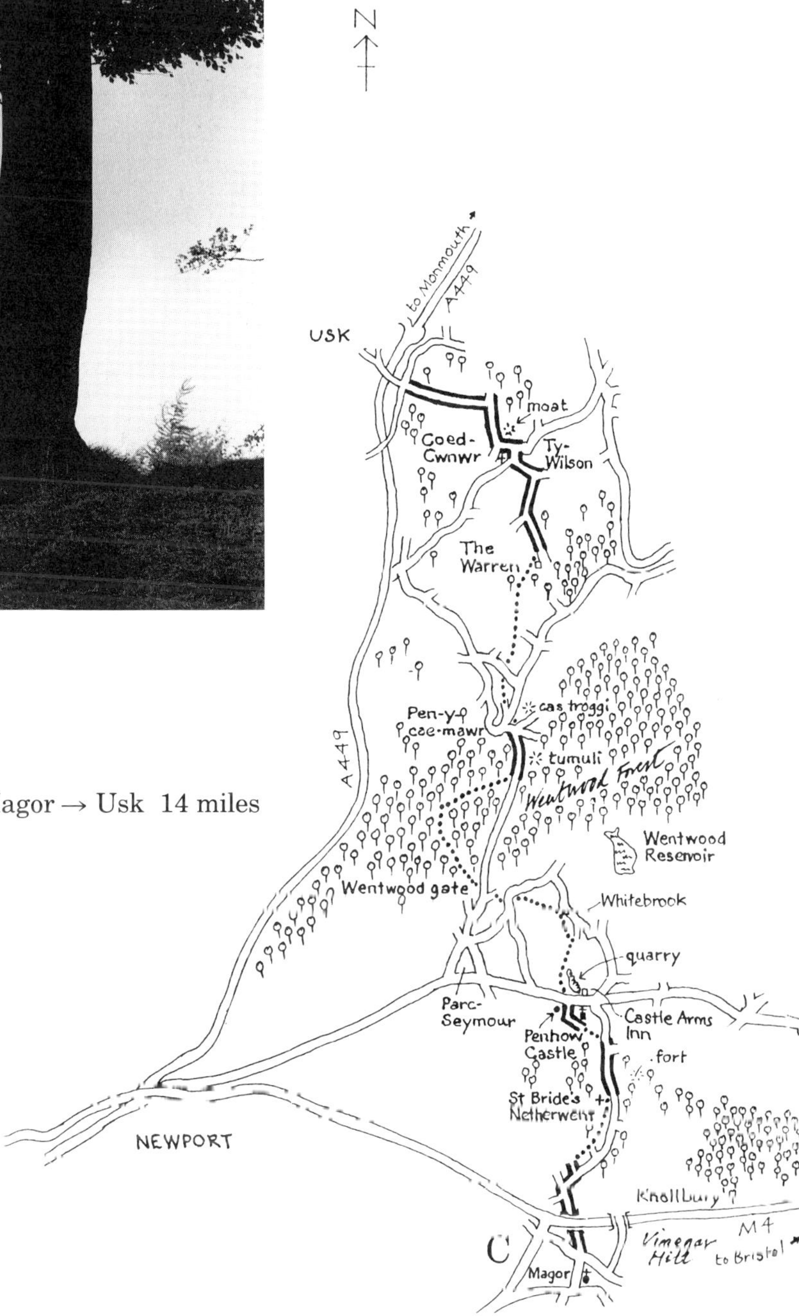

which no doubt provided grazing for the herds passing through this way; but when the inn was re-opened in 1987, it was called by its more recent name.

A footpath goes north beside Rock Farm, taking you by a strip of woodland to the rim of a vast quarry. This way leads to a field, in which I have found a great harvest of mushrooms, and then along a track past a fish farm to Whitebrook (171:421924).

As you go west from here towards Wentwood Gate, you will go along a field-path beside the grounds of a small market garden and then turn left along the lane until you reach the path to your right going north-west to the entrance to the forest. Continue north-west as you follow the old road through the trees, and then turn east along the track that runs through the forest to join the lane at Little Oak.

Follow the lane north from here, turning right by the chapel of Pen-y-caeMawr (171:412950). Past the chapel a field-path on your left follows the course of a long-used farm-track running past a ruined stone building with a yew tree planted beside it, which suggests that this too might once have been a traveller's inn. When you reach a lane, you will find a public footpath sign informing you that it is now two miles to Warren Wood, a message that you will have cause to remember.

The first two-thirds of these two miles is a delight. The way starts off along a narrow path by a mixed woodland where Spanish chestnuts flourish. This brings you to a high ridge, from which you can look westwards to the mountains of Abergavenny and some of the routes that we shall trace in Chapter 9. Another delight of this way, if you have come at the time of year to take advantage of the mushrooms, is the splendour of the pink flush of spindle in the hedgerows.

Enjoy it all you can, for when you reach Warren Wood another prospect daunts. Here, unless things have radically changed since my last visit, you will find that you have to scramble downhill through a shoulder-high nightmare of brambles, which even cover the stile and make progress a slow and painful matter, if not impossible for those without a sharp pair of secateurs or at least a stout stick.

Once you have managed to negotiate the wood, you will find that you have an easy walk along the lane that goes past the Warren, a much modernized farmhouse, towards the hollow-way that runs east to Newchurch from 171:415982. If you want to follow its course, you could use it as a way to join the next walk (see page 165).

To persist on the way to Usk, however, you will need to keep to the lane, turning left at the T junction. At the next road junction (Coed-Cwnwr 171:411991) you will find a large, decayed stone building surrounded by railings to stop you investigating it too closely. From the road, you can make out the date of 1826 engraved over one doorway and the substantial remains of a set of almshouses attached to this former chapel.

It is sad that this place should be so deserted and that despite applications to make it habitable again for homeless young people, the building is being allowed to fall apart. Ironically, the burnt-out shell of Yew Tree Cottage, a pretty little four-square dwelling across the road from the chapel ruins, was being privately restored when I last walked there.

The way to Usk continues along the lane to the north, and at Upper House (171:409999) you will turn left down a narrow hollow-way leading to the bridge across the A449 by the Olway Inn (171:395003). Follow the road towards the town, turning left at the Greyhound Inn, and you will come into Usk via the path that leads through the churchyard. If you go on from there through the square and take the main road towards the river, you will come to signs directing you to the extensively informative Gwent Rural Life museum. An hour or so spent here will give you a good understanding of how the work was done on the farms that we have passed on our walks north from Newport. You will also find a portable forge that might well have been used to replace oxen cues, as the herds journeyed east into England.

D The last walk in this section starts from the medieval walls set up round the Roman city of Venta Silurum (Caerwent) (171:469905), the marketplace of the Celtic Silures. This seems to have been a real meeting place of the two nations, who shared the temple, although there was never any doubt as to who was ultimately in command; it was the Second Augustan Legion that established the Forum and the baths. Excavations are still going on to reveal the foundations of these lost buildings in the town, which later generations of Celts have re-named Caerwent.

The A48, which by-passes the town, follows the course of the Roman road running to the west. To start on our journey from here towards Monmouth, we shall go north across the valley which was a busy thoroughfare long before the legions marched along it, for this was one way to the sea. It continued to be so when the drovers took their cattle this way, for in his *Memoirs of Monmouthshire* (first published in 1708) Nicholas Rogers claimed that 'ships of 500 tuns' came to Chepstow quay. A mile across this valley from Caerwent there is an even older defensive position, the hill fort of Great Llanmellin, set high on a hill so that any unwelcome intruders could be easily observed and intercepted. You reach the woods around those earthworks by the lane that goes north across the valley from the A48 at 171:460907.

Turn north-east from here to Shirenewton, three miles to the west of

D Caerwent → Trelleck 17 miles

E Raglan Castle → Red House Farm 6 miles

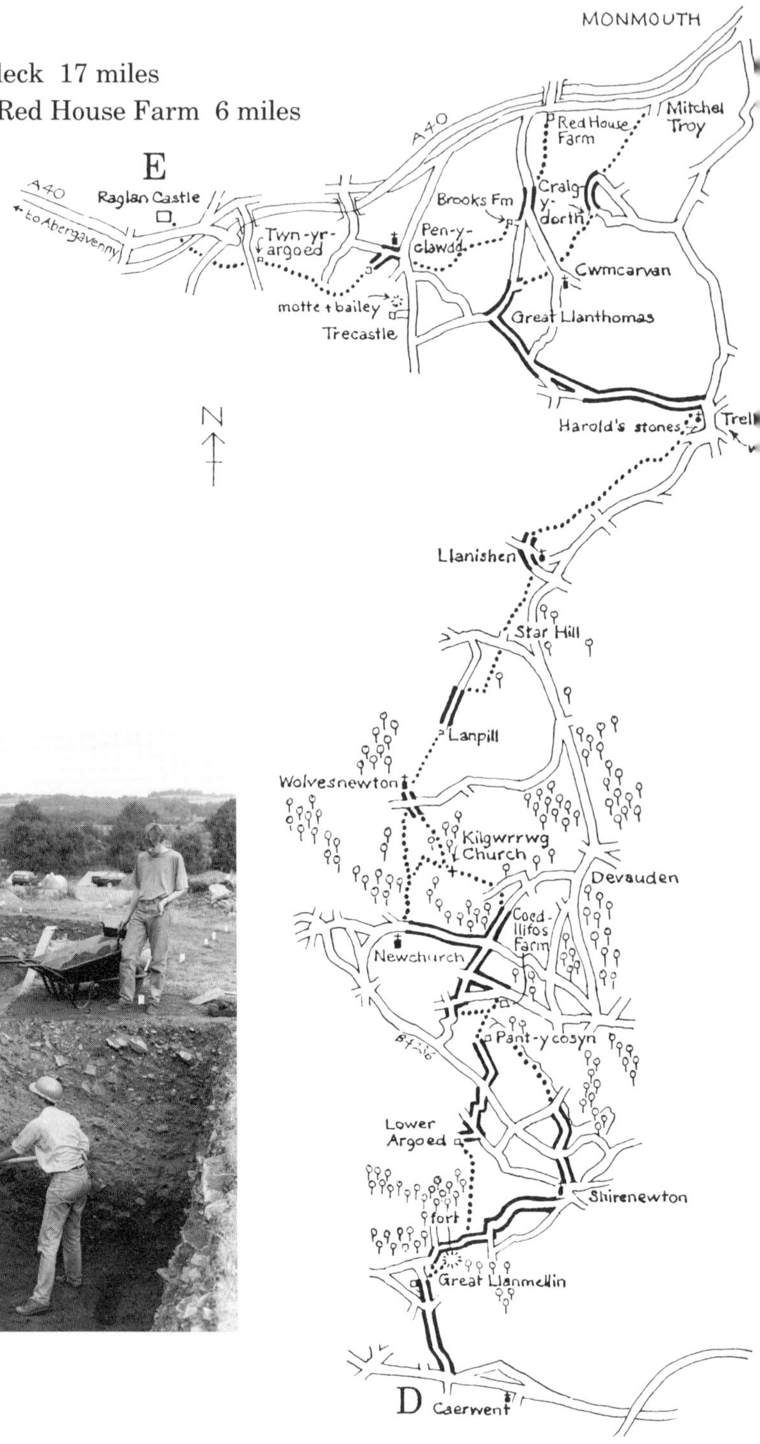

Excavations at Caerwent.

Chepstow, and go north from its great perpendicular church towards the Mountain Brook. A footpath follows the course of that stream along its southern bank to the farm of Pant-y-Cosyn (171:465958). Go north-east from here across the fields to Coed-llifos Farm, and then follow the lanes round to Kilgwrrwg Common. Several paths from here lead to the tiny, isolated church of Kilgwrrwg, set in a circular churchyard, which betokens a pre-Christian origin for the sacred site, a pagan beginning which partly persisted into the Middle Ages to judge by the female fertility figure on the outer west wall.

The simplest way to approach this church is along the lane to the east of the forestry plantation, and then to follow the steep farm-track downhill to Kilgwrrwg House. The more direct way is by the footpath that leaves the road to Newchurch at 171:460975; and you can also get there by starting off along the path that runs between Newchurch and Wolvesnewton.

As you climb the hill here you come to a crossing of the tracks: the way to the east goes to Kilgwrrwg church; the one to the west enters a forest and climbs up to another Iron Age fort enclosed in a double rampart. More pertinent to our travels however is the model farm and agricultural museum (162:445986) on the hillside beneath the prehistoric enclosure. The way ahead goes to Wolvesnewton. From the church here you can take a direct footpath downhill to Lanpill Farm (171:460007), and from there take the tracks past Llanvihangel Court to Star Hill.

Footpaths lead across the fields from here by Duffryn Farm to Llanishen. Take the road going north-east from this village, it will bring you to the path that comes out by the three Harold's stones: eight-foot-high, prehistoric, pudding-stone monoliths that have given their name to the village of Trelleck, that is 'Three Stones' (162:498052). They prove the antiquity of this route, which later became a Roman thoroughfare linking Chepstow, some twelve miles to the south, with Monmouth, five miles to the north. In the Middle Ages, Trelleck was once the largest settlement in Wales: but it started to decline during Llewellyn's rebellion in the thirteenth century; suffered heavily during the outbreaks of plague, including the Black Death, at that time; and was further diminished in the Glendower revolt of 1403. By the seventeenth century no market was held here.

Although for the seventeenth- and eighteenth-century cattle drovers Trelleck was simply a place to pass by or through, pilgrimages were still being made here on account of a healing well. This St Ann's Well (162:504052), also known as the Virtuous Well on account of its properties, can now be found in the corner of a field beside the minor road that runs south-east from the village. Its waters were said to be as

Virtuous Well, Trelleck.

medicinal as those of the more fashionable Tunbridge Wells in Kent. They flow from four springs, three of which contain iron, and each one was assigned to the cure of a particular disease. As the sick waited their turn for a cure, they were able to sit on the stone seats, which now provide the walker with a good resting place.

Harold's Stones at Trelleck.

The route from here to Monmouth starts by going west along the lane that starts at Trelleck church. To reach it you take the footpath beside Court Farm across the road from the standing stones. This will take you past Tump Terret, the forty-foot-high mound on which a wooden castle, set high above its moat, stood from the thirteenth century. The footpath

Chepstow castle.

goes beside it, past an old farmyard and flanked to the left by a field whose mounds suggest the site of the long-vanished, prosperous, medieval village. The lane brings you out where the B4293 curves into the village. Almost immediately you will find a lane to your left.

Follow the signposts to Great Llanthomas about three miles away, and then turn north. In half a mile you will come to a footpath on your right, going across the valley to Cwmcarvan (161:477077). Across the lane north-west of the church, go north over a stream and uphill to Craig-y-dorth. Now follow the lane to the north, and, as it bends round sharply to the right, take the footpath going by the side of a wood and then over the hills to the lane that runs through Mitchel Troy (162:494105) to the B4293, and the entry into Monmouth across the gated Monnow bridge, and from there across the Wye and over the wooded hills of the Forest of Dean to the banks of the Severn and the Gloucester markets.

E Mitchel Troy was also on the route for the herds being driven out of Abergavenny through Raglan. Before starting that walk, you could find that a visit to the walls of Raglan castle will give you a clear view of the terrain across which the herds were driven. To start the walk, leave the lane to the south and east of the castle at Twyn-yr-argoed (161:429077) and take the path across the fields by Ty Harry (161:447077) to Pen-y-Clawdd. At the crossroads to the south of the church here, a path goes across the hill to Brooks Farm (161:470084). When you get to the lane here turn left, and after half a mile take the path from the farm- track to Bailey Glace; it goes north-east past Red House Farm to the lane to Mitchel Troy.

On their route from Monmouth, these herds would have been joined by other cattle bought by the English drovers from the markets around Abergavenny. At Skenfrith, further up the Monnow at 161:456204, according to Charles Hassall writing in 1815, five-year-old horned cattle, who had worked as oxen, were sold in prime condition to the drovers and taken to Gloucester and Bristol markets. We shall trace part of their route in Chapter 10.

Chapter 8

Across the Brecon Beacons

The area that now makes up the Brecon Beacons National Park consists of four distinct regions: the Black Mountain and the headwaters of the Usk in the west (see Chapter 5); Fforest Fawr, the original hunting forest in the centre; the high range, which includes Pen y Fan and which gives its name to the whole park now; and the Black Mountains, which we shall explore in the last two chapters, in the east.

Now we are concerned with the two central regions; as we continue along the route of the Sarn Helen, which we left near Coelbren (see p.134), we shall be crossing an area of moorland that was set aside as a royal hunting forest in the eleventh century by the Norman, Bernard de Neumarch. Six hundred years later there were no deer to be seen in this wilderness, described by Defoe as 'horrid and frightful', nor were there many trees, for it is important to remember that in its original meaning 'forest' indicates a stretch of land set apart from normal land ownership and agricultural use, not a large piece of woodland. So much of it was used for communal grazing of cattle, sheep, ponies and even geese and it still is, except, ironically enough, where forests in our modern meaning of the word have been planted in the form of close-packed acres of conifers.

However there are still wide stretches of open country, often too wet for planting, and these are grazed by cattle, sheep and ponies, as they were when the drovers brought their cattle from the west. It was a matter that must have caused the owners of the animals some difficulty as they tried to keep their own herds and flocks clear of the interlopers.

Some of the Pembrokeshire cattle were sold at Brecon market, which can trace its history back to the fifteenth century. However they do not seem to have been too popular with the local farmers. When John Clark wrote his survey of the county for the Board of Agriculture in 1794, he noted that nobody had given these 'foreign' cattle a fair trial on the Brecon commons, because 'among other reasons they are found troublesome, by a habit of breaking through fences, that would turn back or confine the native breed of the district'. In the nineteenth century, another set of 'foreigners' arrived. These were the swarthy black Galloways, which you can still distinguish on the uplands. They were brought in by the Scottish family of McTurk, who brought their cattle with them when they bought the Crown Forest and set up their estate, based on Cnewr (160:890220).

Flooded marsh at Mynydd Illtyd, Brecon Beacons.

On the slopes of the Brecon Beacons.

John Clark also complained about the number of sheep stealers on these hills, suggesting that the thieves were 'driven to bad acts by idleness'. Idleness — or more positively an increase in leisure — with all its attendant benefits and problems, may not often lead to sheep stealing now, but it does cause considerable problems in the management of a conservation area, which hundreds of thousands of people each year are attracted to visit. From the walker's point of view, it means that these tramps along the drove ways, which naturally follow the driest, clearest paths, are best taken in late autumn or early spring, when at least you can enjoy the illusion of having the hills to yourself.

A The first walk goes along the course of the Sarn Helen, and starts at the village of Tonyfildre (160:863108), just north-east of the Roman fort, where we left the old road in Chapter 6. You will find that the footpath starts just to the south-east of the village and goes to join the Sarn Helen as that road climbs on to the high moor. As you reach the high ground, it is worth turning round to look south across the open-cast mines that halted our walk from the south.

After the climb across the open moor from the Afon Pyrddin to Cefngwaunhynog (160:874115) and the vast forest of Coed y Rhaiadr, whose conifers cover old roads linking lost farms, and at least one Bronze Age cairn, the Sarn Helen coincides with a metalled lane for a few hundred yards. It ends at a cattle grid, and across that, the Roman road runs alongside the dark ranks of the fir trees. So you walk with the wall of the forest to your right, and the desolate, moorland waste on your left.

You enter the forest by an area of waterfalls as a stream hurtles down through the trees towards the River Neath, whose waters you will soon be walking above when the Sarn Helen comes out of the forest and goes north along its eastern edge. At 160:907139 I would advise you to leave the Sarn Helen for a little way, by taking the path that goes north-west through the trees and on to the open moor. On the hillsides you will find a series of 'pillow mounds', warrens where rabbits were farmed from the Middle Ages until the First World War, a form of agriculture that was given an enormous boost under the management of the Cnewr estate in the middle of the nineteenth century. Then a special breed of black rabbit was introduced to these warrens, the meat being sent to the towns and villages that had grown up around the iron works and collieries in the south; the black fur served the London hat trade.

Just uphill from the first set of these mounds, you will come to a place where many tracks meet (160:904146). Take the one on your right. It will bring you back to the edge of the forest and a ford across the River Neath. Now you will be climbing, steeply at first, towards the next plantation of conifers, the area of crags to the south of the path hiding more pillow mounds and the remains of several limekilns.

Just before you enter the next belt of trees, you will find a nine-foot-high standing stone to your right. This is Maen Madoc, surrounded by a platform of flat stones, and bearing an inscription to the Roman Dervac, son of Justus, probably carved on an existing prehistoric monolith. If you go round to the south side of this stone you can just make out some of the letters that are thought to have been carved soon after the Romans left Britain.

If you look north from here, you will see another standing stone marking the Sarn Helen. This is the Bronze Age Maen Llia, which has its name from the valley to the east of it. We shall make our way towards it by walking gradually downhill along a wide track through the forest in order to join the lane that goes north to south through Fforest Fawr.

Turn left along this lane which runs beside the Afon Llia, and then walk north for about a mile. The continuation of our route, probably erroneously still known as the Sarn Helen, branches off to the east across the headwaters of the Llia, when the lane bends slightly to the

Maen Madoc by Sarn Helen.

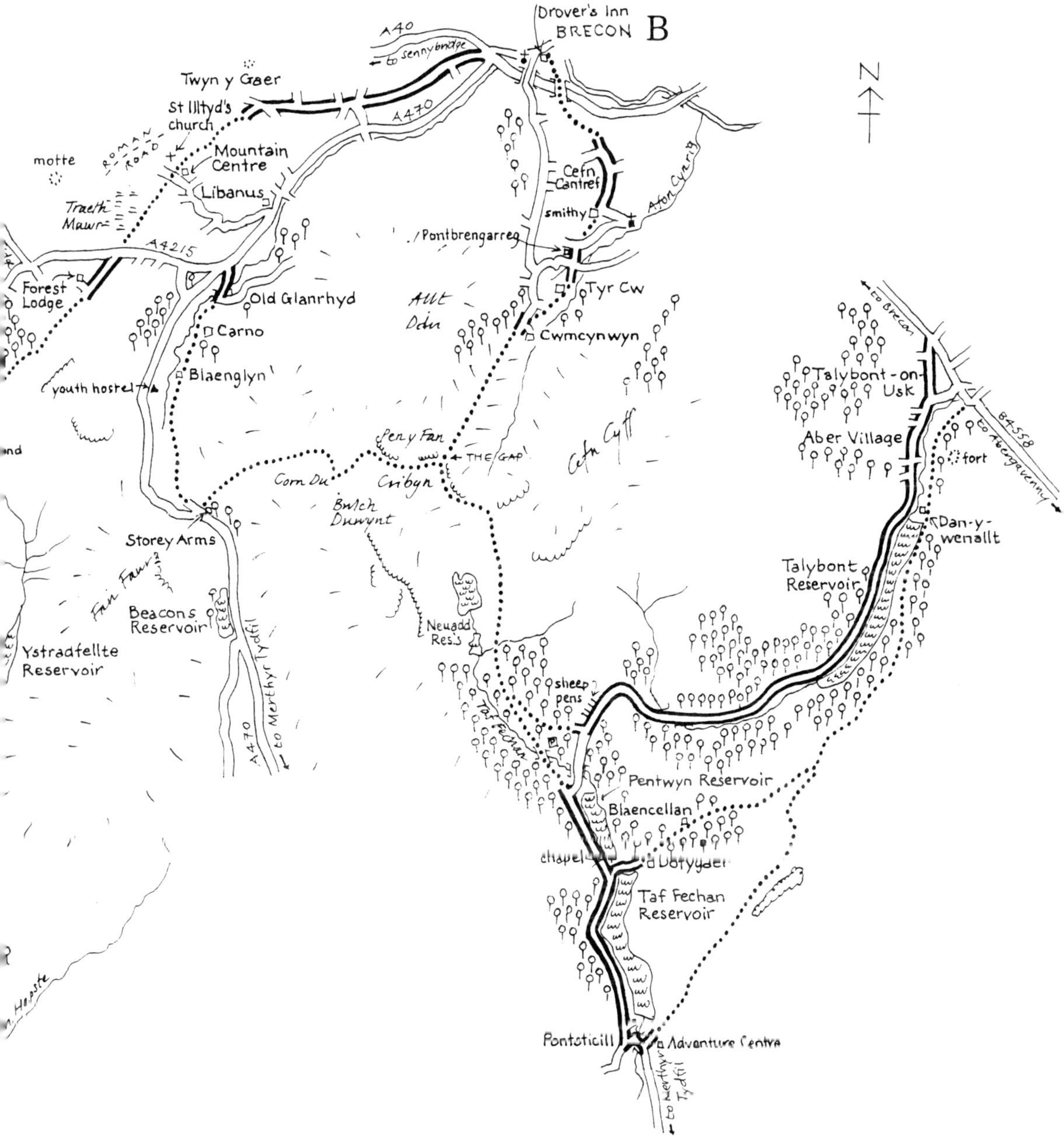

Drover's Inn
BRECON
B
A40
to Sennybridge
Twyn y Gaer
St Illtyd's church
ROMAN ROAD
motte
Mountain Centre
Libanus
A470
Traeth Mawr
A4215
Forest Lodge
Old Glanrhyd
Carno
Blaenglyn
youth hostel
Cefn Cantref
smithy
Afon Cynrig
Pontbrengarreg
Allt Ddu
Tyr Cw
Cwmcynwyn
Pen y Fan
THE GAP
Corn Du
Cribyn
Bwlch Duwynt
Cefn Cyff
Storey Arms
Fan Fawr
Beacons Reservoir
Ystradfellte Reservoir
A470
to Merthyr Tydfil
Neuadd Res's
Taf Fechan
sheep pens
Talybont-on-Usk
Aber Village
fort
to Brecon
B4558
to Abergavenny
Dan-y-wenallt
Talybont Reservoir
Pentwyn Reservoir
Blaencellan
chapel
Dolygaer
Taf Fechan Reservoir
Pontsticill
Adventure Centre
to Merthyr Tydfil

west and starts to climb uphill to the north. The actual course of the Roman road, now lost, went somewhere between the lane and the wide track that we shall follow and which is confidently known as the drovers' road.

This part of the so-called Sarn Helen is sometimes used by farm vehicles, and you will find it worn and muddy, particularly in its early stages. Just before you reach the ford, where the old road meets the headwaters of the Llia, scramble uphill to the standing stone. Maen Llia has served as a waymark for thousands of years, for as we have already noted it occupies a very prominent position, and we shall continue to see it for some distance as we continue north along the drove road. Twelve foot high by nine foot wide, this massive pointed stone, two and a half foot thick in its central area, appears to stand in the middle of a circular

Maen Lia.

cairn, but perhaps this impression comes from the way the top soil has subsided around it.

Back on the pebbled drove road, which runs here by a low wall, and which has definite banks on either side, you head north-east around the contours of the hill above the Senny before making quite a steep descent past the small pool, where cattle could have been watered in a narrow valley. The drove road winds uphill from here, distinctly parting company with the original Roman road, lying below it to the west, its course apparently marked by a bank of hawthorns. There are more hawthorns by the drove route itself, and on the hillside above it; as you climb up from the pool, you will see clumps of pines, which have nothing to do with the forestry conifers. These were planted on the bare hillside as an indication of the route, to show where cattle and sheep might graze, and where their drovers might obtain some refreshment.

Past the farm-track that runs down into the valley on your right, you will again find yourself walking by forestry trees. However these firs do not seem to be so dark and densely packed, for the edges of this forest are happily blurred and softened by the ubiquitous hawthorns. These grow on the edge of a national nature reserve, through which the path runs. It is gated now, and goes through the lower edge of the hillside meadows to join the road at Forest Lodge (160:962244), which leads up to the A4215 and the route across Mynydd Illtyd.

The farm on the further side of the main road was formerly an inn. Here, although the path we are going to walk along is quite clear, the course of the old routes is confused. A bank of hawthorns to the right, as we go through the gate, indicates one vanished track; but the course of the Sarn Helen itself, the Roman road heading straight for the camp to the west of Brecon, is well to the west of our route, and some of the original stones are still discernible at 160:963272, across the lane beyond St Illtyd's church.

The track we are on skirts the marshes that lie to the west of it, and then joins the road running past the National Park's Mountain Centre, a recommended place for anybody who wants to know more about the extent of this wild and perpetually fascinating stretch of country. From here you can look east to the ridge of Pen y Fan and Corn Du, which we shall be approaching in the next walk. Having looked at the mountains across the valley, you can go into the centre to look at the models explaining the glacial formations of this most striking landscape.

The common land of Mynydd Illtyd around the Centre is worth exploring. Across the marshes, at 160:958261, there is a mound indicating the site of a Norman castle, and beside it there is a clear pond, where the drovers could water their animals after the long haul up from the pond we passed well to the south of Forest Gate. Slightly north-west of the Mountain Centre, and on the direct course of the real Sarn Helen, the grassy track that has been cut through the gorse and bracken leads across a lane to Twyn y Gaer, a single rampart hill fort, with yet another 'pillow mound' beside it. That is generally marked as a cairn on the Ordnance Survey maps.

From here the droves heading for Brecon market made their way along the lane that runs north-east, and crossed over the Usk by the town bridge. The cattle market is still on the further side. On their way they went by the Drovers' Inn, which still stands almost opposite the church. This inn would also have served those drovers and farmers who were going south to the growing town of Merthyr Tydfil, the destination of the herds whose route we abandoned by the open cast-mines at Hirwaun at the end of Chapter 6.

An exploration of the routes taken by those southern droves would mean either following the A465 to Cefn-coed-y-cymmer (160:030080); heading north towards Brecon through Penderyn along the A4059; or, more interestingly, going north-east along the lane that led to the farms now submerged beneath the Llwyn-on Reservoir beyond Cadair Fawr, a rugged, rocky mountain, whose lower, eastern slopes still have the platforms of the houses of a medieval settlement. This will be rather a different walk from the one George Borrow made in 1854; he approached what appeared to be a glowing mountain in the south-east, and was in fact the dross from Merthyr's iron forges.

B However, as we have reached the Drovers' Inn at Brecon, it makes more sense to turn directly south from here and walk the Gap road towards Merthyr Tydfil. Beside the gate of Christchurch College, across the road from the Drovers' Inn, you will see a public footpath sign pointing you across the school playing fields. If you follow that path you will join the track that runs east from St David's Hospital and then turns south to climb uphill to Cantref, a mountainous region of scattered farms, where sheep have long been collected from the high summer grazing grounds. This is the start of the route towards the pass beneath Pen y Fan; and as 'the Gap road' has also been claimed as a Roman thoroughfare.

The wide track, from the hospital, will bring you out at the eastern end of the lane along the Cantref ridgeway. At this point the track also gets a metalled surface, and is in fact a continuation of the ridge lane as it turns sharply to the right and starts to go downhill. Here, and for much of your climb up from Brecon, you will be aware of walking towards the shapely and magnificent red sandstone mountains, carved by ice and rising

The Gap road.

majestically above the valley. They cannot fail to beckon you on, and I cannot believe that familiarity would have blurred their impact on the men who drove cattle or walked sheep up this mountain road.

The lane, which is now part of the original track, goes down to the old smithy, now a wood turner's and a weaver's cottage. The course of the original track leaves the lane here, and runs beside the garden of this house; you will see the stile leading to it, clearly waymarked with a broad yellow arrow. As you cross the first field, you can see what has become of the original road from Brecon to the mountains, for the footpath runs close to a hedge above a deep hollow-way, whose banks have been so

worn away that the tree roots are fully exposed. The pebbled surface of the old road, some eight feet below you, now often serves as the bed of a stream. Here the old road may have vanished as a thoroughfare, but at least the legacy of a right of way beside it remains.

The footpath and the old road come together at an ancient crossroads, beneath the massive, stone farm buildings of Pontbrengarreg (160:048249). Our way to the south goes straight ahead; however, if you do not want to continue walking south to Merthyr Tydfil, you could turn east here, along the lane past Cantref church to Llanfrynach, a village in which there was another smithy. From there you could follow the B4558 for a little way to the banks of the Monmouthshire and Brecon canal. A walk east along the towpath will bring you most pleasantly to Talybont and Crickhowell for the drove routes in the next chapter. This route is close to the one advocated by John Clark in his 1794 Board of Agriculture report, in which he advised his readers 'to avoid the horrible precipice' of the road over Bwlch, by keeping to the side of the river Usk.

But back to our route: from the old crossroads, the way to the south goes along the lane past Pontbrengarreg Farm, over the hill and down to the Cynrig river, where a low shelving of the bank on its northern side indicates that a diagonal fording place had once been constructed here. It is now crossed by a small bridge leading to the lane that climbs uphill to a large house set in a clump of pines. This is Tyr Cw (160:045244), and we have reason to suspect from its name that it was another smithy, for *cw* is the word for the half shoe made for the cloven feet of cattle. The old farmhouse is now an informal art gallery. Beside it a narrow, overgrown, stony, sunken lane, clearly a continuation of our original track, climbs up to the lane by Cwmcynwyn Farm.

At the end of that lane, a gate opens on to the open mountains and the rocky path that runs along the eastern flank of Bryn-teg, above the green valley of the Cynwyn, whose waters spring from the marshy ground beneath the cliffs to the south. As you come through the gate onto this path, you will see more pines planted by the wayside, route indicators to thousands of travellers, and possibly a suggestion that shelter and grazing could be had at the farm nearby. Long before they were planted, people were making use of this route, which was certainly in existence long before the Romans or even the Celts came to find a way through the high Brecon escarpment, whose summits form the Beacons.

It is a gentle, if rough, track you are on now, but it becomes much steeper as you near the narrow pass between the ridges of Craig Cwm Cynwyn to the west and Cwm oergwm to the east. It is very rocky here, and only the presence of some ponies on the hillside makes it possible to believe that animals were driven this way.

By the Gap road.

Above Cwm Cynwyn.

Obviously the high ridges themselves cannot be part of a droving story, although if you are lucky enough to ride along them (see end of this chapter), you will get a splendid view of the whole terrain and the possible routes across it. If you are on foot, and find the heights irresistible, you could enjoy the same overall view by joining the Gap road by way of the summits of Corn Du, Pen y Fan and Cribyn. If you do that you will have to travel along the A470, but you will also have a chance to explore the old road which ran south from Libanus, across the Tarell from the A470. You will reach it from the lane that leaves that main road at 160:987248, and goes gently downhill to cross the river at Old Glanrhyd.

Before 1830, when the main road was built, the lane that you are walking on was a coach road, and one of the cottages that you walk by used to be an inn in the late eighteenth century. Further along the lane, you can look up towards Carno Farm, where a building has stood on the hillside since the Middle Ages. It too has Scots pines planted around it, an indication that it also offered beer, shelter and grazing to the drovers. Although cars can be driven quite a good way along this lane, it is usually a quiet place to walk, for it is a 'No through road' and only on foot can you go through the gates leading to the farmland of Blaenglyn (160:987227), a seventeenth-century farmhouse, whose lands are now managed by the National Trust. Just before you reach it you will pass Coed Herbert, a mixed woodland planted on the slope of the hill in memory of Robin Herbert, who was deputy chairman of the Countryside Commission from 1971-80.

Once past the farm the lane becomes a footpath, winding uphill towards Storey Arms. This was never an inn, but a farm named after the landowner, Storey Maskelyne. The inn was actually at Pont ar Daf to the south, and this has completely disappeared, whereas Storey Arms served first as a Youth Hostel and now as an outdoor pursuits centre. It was here that the nineteenth-century drovers who had hoped, by taking the back lane, to avoid the toll charges on the new road found themselves confronted by a demand for payment as they joined the only possible route to Merthyr Tydfil.

If you have gone this way, and now want to join the route south from Cantref, you can take the long, steep path up to Corn Du, Pen y Fan and Cribyn, before climbing down to the southern entrance to the Gap pass. Although no one suggests that any drovers came this way, there are sheep grazing high on the hillsides, and these are still collected and taken down to their winter, lowland pastures at the end of the summer. Eighty years ago, sheep were taken along mountain roads to their winter quarters. The 'taking' journey might last several days, the flock

The road to the Gap.

being penned overnight at a cost of half a crown per hundred sheep.

There are even cairns on the summits of these three peaks, to prove that the red, ridge path, now so severely worn by continuous streams of walkers, was known to Bronze Age people. On your way to the high escarpment from Storey Arms, you will pass the pathetic obelisk to five-year-old Tommy Jones, who was lost on the mountain in August 1900 on his way to visit relations at Cwm-llwych (160:005237): a reminder that although this route is now so much frequented, the climb should not be lightly undertaken.

From Cribyn, the eroded track takes you down to the Gap, and now you join the main route to the south (see p. 181), a pleasant path along the hillside with sufficient worked stones among the turf to indicate that the track was important enough to have been paved at some stage; although it is doubtful whether Roman engineers were responsible for the rounded curbs. It is certain, however, that this way has been known for millennia. In the valley beneath you, the waters of the Neuadd reservoirs (built at the time of the Zulu wars, and once named after them) have drowned Bronze Age cairns, burial places of people familiar with the Gap highway.

The hillside track ends with a steep scramble across the upper waters of the Taf Fechan, and the forestry path on its southern bank. In extremely muddy weather that can be avoided by taking the track down to the reservoir weirs, and then walking a little way south along the lane to join the forestry path as it emerges from the trees, curves south-east along the hillside to join the lane that runs towards Talybont reservoir, and comes into Talybont village through Aber. If you go that way you will find sheep pens placed where the track from the Gap joins the lane.

When you reach Talybont, you can either take the canal towpath to the west, or cross the Usk to the A40, about three miles from Bwlch and the walks in the next chapter.

There are two other ways to complete the Gap walk. One starts across the bridge over the Taf Fechan reservoir, by the chapel at 160:058144 and then goes up to the farm of Blaencellan (160:067150). From there a bridleway goes over the hills up to the forest on the east bank of the Talybont reservoir. The other way is longer, reaching the forest path from a starting point further to the south.

For this route, you follow the lane down to the south of the Taf Fechan reservoir, cross over the dam and then turn south again for a few yards. You will then soon come to a 'No throughway' on your left, going uphill past an adventure centre. From here your way goes along an uphill woodland, rocky path past the ruins of a substantial house to a gate leading out onto the open hills. When you reach the Talybont forest from

Sheepfolds by the road from Taf Fechan.

(*Overleaf, left*) Neuadd Reservoir.

(*Overleaf, right*) Looking north to the Beacons.

here, you will find that you are walking through the trees above the course of the old railway line.

Keep to this upper track, when you come to a short gap in the trees by the dam at the northern end of the reservoir. For a brief while it becomes a forestry road before entering the trees again to the north. Before your view is hidden by the forest, look down at the farmhouse in the valley. This is Dan-y-wenallt uchaf, now Powys's outdoor education centre, a place which runs special walkers' week-ends, and which makes a fine base for anyone wanting to explore the routes in this chapter in more detail. Back among the trees, you will find the path to Talybont, quite narrow now, running parallel to the old railway track, which goes through private land. Path and railway join by the highly arched, cobbled bridge that crosses the Monmouthshire and Brecon canal and leads into Talybont village.

Riding Stables and bridlepaths
Mrs Evans
Cantref Trekking Centre
Upper Cantref
Cantref
Brecon
Powys
LD3 8LR
Llanfrynach (087486 223)
These stables are situated at a farm to the south of Brecon in an area in which the cattle were collected to be driven to the markets in the east, and from which farm produce went over the mountains to Merthyr Tydfil.

Full day rides from here take you along Bryn-teg and Cefn Cyff, the ridges to the west and east of the Gap path; and from the Cwmcynwyn Gate at the entrance to the Gap path and east into the next valley, returning by way of Llanfrynach. Another ride goes from Cwmgwdi (160: 027256) along Cefn Cwm llwch leading towards Pen y Fan and then turning west beneath the main peaks of the park.

There is also a ride beside the canal from Llanfrynach past Talybont to Crickhowell.

Chapter 9

The Black Mountains

Most of the cattle and sheep that were gathered together at Cantref were driven along the Usk valley to Abergavenny, and then east to Monmouth and Gloucester along the route from Raglan castle that we traced in Chapter 7. In this chapter we shall look at alternative northern drove-ways, heading towards Hereford, and approaching the Wye across the hills to the east of Llangorse, and going over the Black Mountains to Talgarth and Hay.

The Black Mountains are a world apart; a wild, remote terrain rising to 2,700 feet and extending some eight miles west to east and ten from north to south. They include the hills to the west of the Rhiangoll valley (where the A479 links Tretower to Talgarth) and reach east to the A465 which runs by Llanvihangel Crucorney and Pandy to Hereford.

In his last novel, Raymond Williams, who was born at Pandy (161: 335219), likens the area to a right hand spread out to the south. Six rivers run between the fingers and along the outside of the thumb, and between them are high ridges with a few isolated farms on the hillsides. Here you can trace the old drove routes to the markets at Hay and Talgarth, and then east across the border to England.

Farmers have grazed sheep on these hill-tops and sown crops in the valleys since the Bronze Age, and you will come across many marks left by those early people. Here, mechanized agricultural methods seem to have had less effect on patterns of farming than we find elsewhere. You will see how the valley farms make use of every scrap of possible pasture; and groups of ponies graze among the bracken. Some of their ancestors were crossed with Arabs when the Romans pressed west to Brecon.

A I shall start this exploration with such a Roman road. It runs from the marching camp at Tretower to cross the Black Mountains' most westerly ridge running north from Bwlch. We shall start from Tretower (161:184214), whose beautifully preserved, medieval manor house, now

in the care of CADW, was the family home of the Vaughans, and frequently visited by the metaphysical poet Henry Vaughan (1621-1695), who spent most of his life at Tynewydd near Scethrog to the west of Llansantffraed, where he is buried. To the west of this courtyard house at Tretower, the Norman keep of the old castle stands guard at the entrance to a wide, wet and fertile valley.

From the lane to the west of this round tower, a path goes across the marshy meadow to the banks of the Yw, a stream that is supposed to have sprung out of the ground beside a single yew tree at Llwyfen (161:157214), and which flows east to join the Rhiangoll. On its way it goes south of Pen-y-gaer, the Roman fort, now only discernible as a faint outline on the green pastures. Here you cross the lane to follow the waymarked paths across the fields to Tre-graig, a beautifully restored, ancient farmhouse. There was a building here when Tretower castle was still standing, and probably long before that. Its home paddock covers a Roman aqueduct.

Go through the former farmyard to the north-east of the house, and you will come again to the clearly marked footpath signs. Take the one that points uphill to the west, and immediately you will find yourself on a well defined old road running between steep banks crowned with ageing trees. It will bring you to a lane, across which it continues over the open hillside as a stony track, grooving its way to the boundary wall that marks the top of the ridge. From here you can look west to the Brecon Beacons and the forests and pastures around Llangorse Lake.

If you want to make a circular walk, turn south-west along this ridge, passing a small cairn and the steep, rutted path that descends to the lanes above Bwlch. To return to Tre-graig, turn east along the lane at the foot of the path, and, just before you reach the cattle-grid and the open hillside, take the much overgrown footpath that winds downhill. It will bring you out by Tyle Cottage and the lower lane to Tre-graig.

Our main route, however, goes to the north along the wide track by the boundary wall. Follow it until you come to a place where a path branches off to your right and makes a steep zig-zag down the hill to the east. This descent starts from a point mid-way between two cairns to the south and the triangulation point to the north. You will pass another Bronze Age cairn halfway down the hillside.

This path will bring you to the farm of Blaenau-draw (161:174265) and from there you can either carry on to the east down the lane that leads to the Rhiangoll valley at Pont Waun-fach, or take the track that runs along the western contour of Cockit Hill, above Cwm Sorgwm. Both routes will lead you to an exploration of the droves across the river.

The Black Mountains by Y Grib.

I will begin with the first alternative. The lane from Blaenau-draw

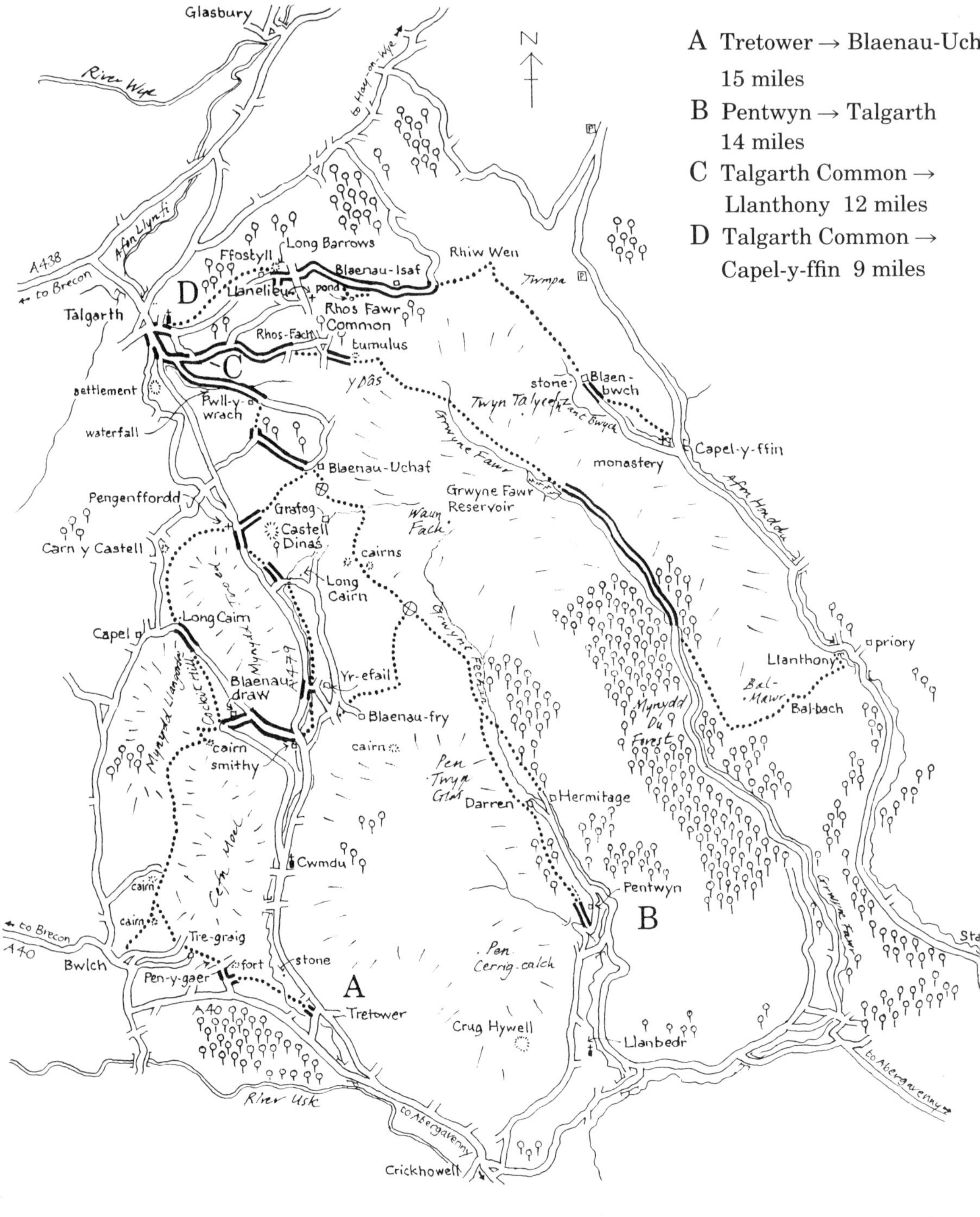
A Tretower → Blaenau-Uch
15 miles
B Pentwyn → Talgarth
14 miles
C Talgarth Common →
Llanthony 12 miles
D Talgarth Common →
Capel-y-ffin 9 miles
N
Glasbury
River Wye
to Hay-on-Wye
Afon Llynfi
A438
to Brecon
Talgarth
Ffostyll
Long Barrows
Llanelieu
pond
Blaenau-Isaf
Rhiw Wen
Twmpa
Rhos Fawr
Common
Rhos-Fach
tumulus
Y Dâs
settlement
Pwll-y-wrach
waterfall
stone
Blaen-bwch
Twyn Talycefn
Nant Bwch
Capel-y-ffin
monastery
Afon Honddu
Blaenau-Uchaf
Grwyne Fawr
Grwyne Fawr Reservoir
Pengenffordd
Grafog
Castell Dinas
Waun Fach
Carn y Castell
cairns
Long Cairn
Long Cairn
Capel
Mynydd Troed
A479
Yr-efail
Blaenau-draw
Blaenau-fry
Mynydd Llangorse
Cockit Hill
cairn
smithy
cairn
Pen Twyn Glas
Darren
Hermitage
Grwyne Fechan
priory
Llanthony
Bal-Mawr
Bal-bach
Mynydd Du Forest
Cefn Moel
Cwmdu
cairn
cairn
Tre-graig
Pentwyn
B
to Brecon
A40
Bwlch
Pen-y-gaer
fort
stone
A
Tretower
A40
Pen Cerrig-calch
Crug Hywell
Llanbedr
River Usk
to Abergavenny
to Abergavenny
Crickhowell
Grwyne Fawr
C
D

reaches the main road (A479) at an acute-angled turn by a bridge across the Rhiangoll. You will notice that this lane has very wide verges, indicating that it was used as a drove-way; to confirm that you will find a forge (now used as a craft workshop) beside the stream that flows into the Rhiangoll by the bridge.

Across the main road a footpath will take you to a lane, follow it uphill to a cross-roads and then turn left to the farm of Yr-efail. If you go north from here, keeping to the east bank of the river, you will find yourself walking on the old cobbled mill lane that runs to the Long Cairn by Cwmfforest (161:183291). Turn left here past a large, long-distance pony-trekking centre; when the lane bends towards the river carry straight on along a continuation of the mill lane, going past the farm of Panteg to the Castle Inn at Pengenffordd.

As an alternative to following the mill lane from Yr-efail, you can go straight uphill along the steep and stony track just west of Blaenau-fry (161:194267). There you will cross a cattle grid and climb up towards the ridge of Mynydd Llysiau. You will join it at a pass where several routes converge, and which is part of the old road between Crickhowell and Talgarth that we shall follow in a later walk. To reach Cwmfforest Long Cairn from here take the track going west from this narrow pass.

Another way to reach Pengenfford is to go across Mynydd Troed to the west of the Rhiangoll. If you have taken the track round Cockit Hill, it will have brought you out to the lane that crosses the hills by another Long Cairn. As you turn left along this lane you will see three boundary stones, the largest of which is inscribed 'Mrs Macnamara 1837'. She was the widow of John Macnamara, owner of a vast estate, covering both sides of the Rhiangoll valley. He might well have lost it if it had not been for his careful wife, for when he died in 1818, a member of the notorious Hell Fire Club in West Wycombe, Buckinghamshire, he was a renowned and profligate rake. In 1796, he built the Hermitage in the depths of the Grwyne Fechan valley in order to install his mistress close at hand. We shall pass the blasted shell of that love-nest, and the carriageway leading up to it on a further walk in this chapter.

The burnt-out Hermitage in the Black Mountains.

The path that you are on will take you north on the western slopes of Mynydd Troed, and, if you look over the valley from here, you will see, as you walk, a network of lanes and footpaths along which cattle and sheep were driven to the market in Talgarth. You will leave the hill just to the east of the earthwork of Carn y Castell (161.158297), following the path past Whitelow Farm to Pengenffordd church.

From the telephone box to the north of the Castle Inn, a lane runs up to Dinas Farm, beneath the hill-top earthworks and crumbling stones of Castell Dinas. There is no official right of way to this extensive Iron Age

The earthworks of Castle Dinas.

(*Right*) Folds of the Black Mountains from Castle Dinas.

fort, but the farmer usually permits access, and it is well worth making the detour to visit it. For in addition to the multiple deep, prehistoric ramparts, you will find Norman masonry, and the remains of a twelfth-century motte and bailey standing at 1,476 feet, the highest castle site in Wales.

Back at Dinas Farm, follow the wide muddy track that comes out at the lane by Blaenau Uchaf (161: 187313), a place where you will also arrive if you follow the next walk tracing the old market road from Crickhowell to Talgarth.

B

The old road follows the course of the lane from Crickhowell through Llanbedr and branches away from it at Cwm Banw, just before reaching the farm of Pentwyn (161:238234). If you have driven along the lane, you can park at the layby just after you have crossed the Banw, a tributary of the Grwyne Fechan. There is a footpath sign here directing you straight up the hillside, but you will get more of a feel of the old road if you walk a little way up the lane and follow the next sign. It will send you through a farmyard and right on to the old road, still cobbled and running between high banks. You then come to a gate leading up to the open hill, and now the wider track curves round to the ridge on your left. Do not follow it, but keep to the path running alongside the wall on your right. This will bring you to a gate leading into a conifer forest. Here, the old way becomes somewhat confused with the wide, new forestry roads which overwhelm it. However the footpath signs are clear, and if you follow their apparently improbable route, you will come clear of the trees and find yourself on a wide grassy track, running through the bracken, above some ruined farm buildings.

This lovely, green ribbon goes along the western slopes of the Grwyne Fechan valley to join John Macnamara's carriageway to the Hermitage. If you follow that, you will find that you cross the river by a charming, grassed-over stone bridge (161:223262). Across the valley the green carriageway will bring you to the forestry road, and you will see the gloomy shell of the Hermitage on your left as you go downhill. There is no trace of romance there now, the conifers have seen to that; but to be fair the place was always more grand than pretty and quite inappropriate to the majesty of the surrounding hills. In the late nineteenth century, it served as an opulent shooting lodge for Lord Glanusk, and a picture of it survives in Richard Baker-Gabb's *Hills and Vales of the Black Mountains* published in 1913.

The main route of the old road keeps to the west side of the valley, climbing gradually among the grazing ponies to the pass at 161:204287, making a sharp zig-zag through the protruding rocks to get there. This pass is the point that you will have reached, if you went east from Blaenau-fry in the last walk. The ridge here stretches south to Pen Twyn Glas, and north to Pen Trumau, where it curves east to Waun Fach, the highest point in the Black Mountains. At the pass you will see the tempting track going down the hillside to Cwmfforest, but your way goes north, between the two cairns on the hillside beneath Pen Trumau. If these Bronze Age cairns were ever turfed over, their stones have long been left bare. They are great mounds, and some enterprising shepherd has made use of them by constructing small shelters from the stones on the east side of each cairn to provide protection from the prevailing winds.

The old road from Crickhowell to Talgarth, near Talymaes.

Llanbedr bridge.

Once past the second cairn, you will look in vain for any clearly marked way; instead you will be confused by a mass of thread-like paths and sheep-runs criss-crossing the boggy upland. The clearest route runs steeply downhill to the valley farms. If you follow it, turn right at the bottom and make your way above the edges of the fields to the stepping stones that cross the upper waters of the Rhiangoll (161: 197304).

A more dramatic way to reach that place involves a fairly tricky descent, for if you continue at the upper level, you will find as you round

Hills above Talgarth.

the hillside that the slope gets steeper and more and more difficult to negotiate. It is hard to work out how the old Talgarth road could ever have got to this river-crossing, for now the steep hillside is almost entirely covered in scree, roughly held in place by a few patches of bilberries. Yet the ford at the bottom of the hill indicates that this was once a well-used route.

Across the river the path is clear again, curving up to the pass below Y Grib, and then winding down to Blaenau-Uchaf. When you reach the lane, turn left past a ruined farmhouse; and when the lane turns sharply to the left at Rhos Farm (161:175318), take the track on the right. It is signed to a gliding club, but you will find that there is a footpath here, bringing you to another lane by Pwll-y-wrach (161:176323). You can either turn left here along the lane to Talgarth, or continue north-east across the hills to Rhos Fach (161:187334) and the beginning of the next walk.

Hawthorn on Talgarth Common.

Black Mountains from Talgarth Common.

C This walk starts from Talgarth Common, a wide expanse of open, rather marshy moorland intersected by wide-verged lanes, some of which have now been metalled over. You will reach such an intersection of lanes if you follow the path due east from Rhos Fach. If you should come this way in late spring, you will be greeted here by a stunning wide avenue of pink hawthorn leading up to the open moor; this route is now more generally associated with the men who worked on creating the Grwyne Fawr reservoir from 1890 to 1926 than with the drovers and shepherds. Yet because the high ridges of the Black Mountains can often be more boggy than the valleys, it is possible that the cattle were sometimes taken this way, and sheep most certainly were.

In any case, there is a steep climb ahead before you reach the Grwyne Fawr valley, and you start it by walking along this lovely wide, hawthorn-flanked grassy road. At the further end the contour lines come close together as the path seems to go almost vertically up Y Das and on to the high moor. Here you will come to a meeting place of wider

On Talgarth Common.

tracks; the one to your left, which has climbed up to this point from the other side of the narrow cleft in the hill you have been walking beside, is the Rhiw Cwmstabl that started from the pond in the middle of Rhos Fawr Common, which we can visit in the course of the last walk in this chapter. The Rhiw Cwmstabl was the main route for the men working on the reservoir, being a slightly shorter and easier climb than the one we have undertaken. Nevertheless they were no doubt glad to find refreshment at the Six Bells, an inn long disappeared, but which had a flourishing trade on this route during the nineteenth century. If you go out of your way by turning north along the Rhiw Cwmstabl, and follow that track downhill to the awkward rocky steps at 161:200334, you will find the names of some of the men who worked on the reservoir cut into a boulder.

The main route to the south from the intersection at the top of the escarpment goes across the open moor, along the track that those men tramped to work each day. It is now a ramblers' highway, and as worn as ever it was when the reservoir was being built. This path begins a gentle descent to cross the infant Grwyne Fawr that feeds the reservoir, and from this place it is a pleasant easy walk for a couple of miles to that wide stretch of water in the valley. In wet weather, you will be glad to find the old disused meter house by the edge of the reservoir, it makes a good dry shelter in which to eat your sandwiches.

The dam at the southern end of the reservoir is 153 feet high, and from here you will find a metalled road leading into the Mynydd Du (Black Mountain) Forest and a Forestry Commission picnic place at Blaen-y-cwm (161:254284). On a site now lost among the trees to the west of that place, some of the reservoir workers lived in the vanished Navvyville — a temporary workmen's settlement.

More pertinent to our story are the numbers of sheepfolds marked on old maps and now wiped out by the conifer plantations; and the farms that have been similarly drowned in fir trees. There was one such sheepfold at 161:248289, just across the river from the lane as it enters the forest. More sheepfolds were marked around the lost farm of Nant-ybedd (161:255268), by the forest road to the west of the lane; and at Blaen-y-cwm (161:254284), which you will pass just before the lane crosses the river, a sheep-wash or dipping place once important enough to be marked on the map of 1905, which also shows further sheepfolds on the steep, western slopes of the Grwyne Fawr valley.

Soon after passing Blaen-y-cwm, you can leave the lane for the path going south-east out of the trees and onto the open hillside. Follow this way round to the south for about a mile until you reach a junction of tracks just before the crossing of a stream. Keep to the way on your left. This track curves east before starting to climb round the southern edge of the ridge which stretches from Twyn Tal y Cefn (161:224324) in the north to Bal-Mawr (161:268271) in the south. From this height, you will go down the steep, open, green hillside to the lane across the Afon

Honddu from the ruins of Llanthony Priory, and one of the routes into England, which we shall follow in the next chapter.

D The final walk following the droves over the Welsh Black Mountains starts from St Gwendoline's church in Talgarth, where a large black slab commemorates the conversion in Lent 1735, experienced by Howell Harris, evangelist and agricultural reformer, who later set up a Christian farming community at Trefeca (161:144321) across the fertile valley to the west of Mynydd Troed. Long before that occurrence there was a pilgrim route from here to Llanthony Priory, and we start this walk by following it to the east of the church, along a tree-lined avenue that leads through Park Wood and then goes along the hillside to Ffostyll Long Barrows (161:178349). Here you can either continue east along the lane which borders Rhos Fawr Common to the north, or make a diversion to the south by farm-track and field-path to the church of Llanelieu (161:185342). It is worth seeking out the key from the farm across the road for the sake of the rough-hewn wooden screen across the chancel – a rare survival.

From the Ffostyll Long Barrow you can make your way east to the pond in the middle of Rhos Fawr Common, and then follow one of the tracks going north-east to join the lane near the valley farm of Blaenau-Isaf (161:201344). From there follow the lane out of the valley to the east and, when it turns sharply to the left, carry on along the path that climbs diagonally up the northern escarpment of the Black Mountains, an outstandingly impressive geographical feature, seeming to rise to a far greater height than it actually does. You will certainly believe that you are climbing a good deal more than a thousand feet as the path turns to the north and rises at an alarmingly acute angle to the high ground beneath the Twmpa or Lord Hereford's Knob (161:225350).

This walk does not take you up to the Twmpa and the ridge of Darren Lwyd, instead you turn south-west to follow one of the most beautiful of valley paths, starting from 161:221347. The path goes along the course of the Nant Bwch (a tributary of the Honddu) for a mile or so to Blaen-bwch farm (161:238328). On a fine spring day, I can think of no better place to be, always within the sound of running water, and with a few outcrops of interestingly shaped grey rocks to diversify the smooth green of the hillsides.

You are making for the little church at Capel-y-ffin, four miles to the north of Llanthony Priory, but there is no need to go along the lane to get there. So turn left when the farm-track joins the lane. This route will take you past some more farm buildings and on to the track that links them with a house on the further side of a wood. From there you cross a field, which I've known to produce splendid rings of mushrooms, and come out on the lane above the tiny church.

This intersection of lanes draws many summer visitors, and has become a popular meeting place for walkers setting out to explore these hills. In the 1920s, it was also, for a short while, the focus of a rather different sort. A rather strange Christian sect established themselves on the hillside, and their house still merits the title of 'monastery' on the Ordnance Survey maps (161:253314).

For some years, Eric Gill, graphic artist and well-known typographer, lived and worked here with many protestations of religious fervour, now somewhat undermined by the revelations from his diaries in a recent biography. Still, nothing can diminish the grandeur of the ridge above the 'monastery', and if you decide to climb up to it, you take a zig-zag path to the cairn-marked heights and the path running south-east to Bal Mawr.

Riding Stable
Sandra Cooke
Longhouse Liveries and Riding Centre
Priory Wood
Clifford
Herefordshire
HR3 5HL
04973 527
Rides from this stable also cover routes in Chapter 10.

Chapter 10

Into England

The drovers whom we have been following from south-west Wales were mostly bound for the Hereford and Gloucester markets. Their route lay through the uneasy country of the Welsh Marches, which for centuries have been much more Welsh than English, and where Welsh law generally prevailed. This borderland is largely defined by the Wye and the Severn, and the crossing of these two major rivers was the main consideration in taking the Welsh cattle to the English markets.

Wherever possible, the drovers naturally wished to choose routes that would allow them to keep clear of toll bridges and the roads maintained by the turnpike trusts. As we shall see, this was not always easy to do, nor is it an easy matter, in the case of the Wye, for us to conjecture just where the crossings could be made: for the course of the river and the extent of its flood bed were quite different when the drovers came here in the seventeenth and eighteenth centuries from the meandering Wye, tamed by catchment control, that we speculate about in our walks. For instance, in 1660 the flood was so great that Glasbury church on the north bank (161:178391) was swept away; and in 1720, the rush of water so changed the course of the river that the old church at Whitney was completely cut off from the village. We can be more confident about the Severn, for the bridge by Over (162:817196) leading to Gloucester's West Gate was the closest crossing to the mouth of the river until the M4 suspension bridge was built.

I shall look first of all at the routes to the Hereford market and the crossings of the Wye that led to it. Two Roman roads once converged on that city from the north and the west. Along the one from the north (now the A4110 and more properly referred to as the Portway), the herds from north and mid-Wales were driven south from Kington. Their story does not belong to this book, but some of the herds whose journeys we have been following may have joined them at Bush Bank (149:452514). A barn behind the Bush Inn here is said to have been used by the drovers.

It stands in a caravan park, and is now full of memorabilia of the old railway, which for a short while did its own share of carrying goods to the Hereford markets.

It would be natural to think that any of the drovers who were heading slightly north of east after they crossed the Wye would have converged on Weobley (149:402518); but that proud town would have none of them, setting toll gates at each end of the main street to keep them out. However, in the seventeenth century, when the castle, now a series of moulded earthworks partly enclosed by the traces of the moat, stood guard over the town, things may well have been different. Then the cattle, driven across the Wye when a dry summer made the ford, twenty yards downstream from the present toll bridge, a viable route, could well have been taken for fattening on the slopes of Burton Hill in order to provision the lord of the castle and his garrison of retainers. However, in later years, the cattle were probably collected on the open space of Weobley Marsh for the final stage of their journey. The whole area is a network of little lanes, several of which show signs of having once been drove routes.

Most of the cattle that were driven across the northern part of the Black Mountains from the markets at Talgarth must have reached Hereford by a more direct route; and their drovers would have tried to avoid tolls by keeping south and west of the Wye as long as possible. They had several possibilities. They could have crossed at Clock Mills (148:292454), where there was another ford crossing to the drovers' inn and shoeing station at Winforton; they could have gone over Merbach Hill to Bredwardine; or by carrying on through Moccas and Preston-on-Wye made the crossing at Bridge Sollers.

A A good starting point for looking at these routes is the Royal Oak Inn at Hardwicke (148:271437). This was once a cider house, and the Scots pine planted beside it could well be a sign that it was once a drovers' inn. From here a wide track goes north through Windle Park and across the B4352, where it becomes a field-path leading to Upper Castleton Farm and the lanes that go to Clock Mills by way of the substantial traces of a motte and bailey.

In this village you will find drinking pools by the side of the road, a sure sign that cattle were driven this way. From the inn on the B4352, an overgrown lane climbs up to the tiny hamlet of Middlewood, where you turn left down the rocky lane that leads on to Merbach Hill. On the summit of this hill, which rises to some 1,000 feet, lush green pasture still provides grazing for cattle and horses. The ways divide here. One route goes south-east to Crafta Webb (148:314444); that is the most

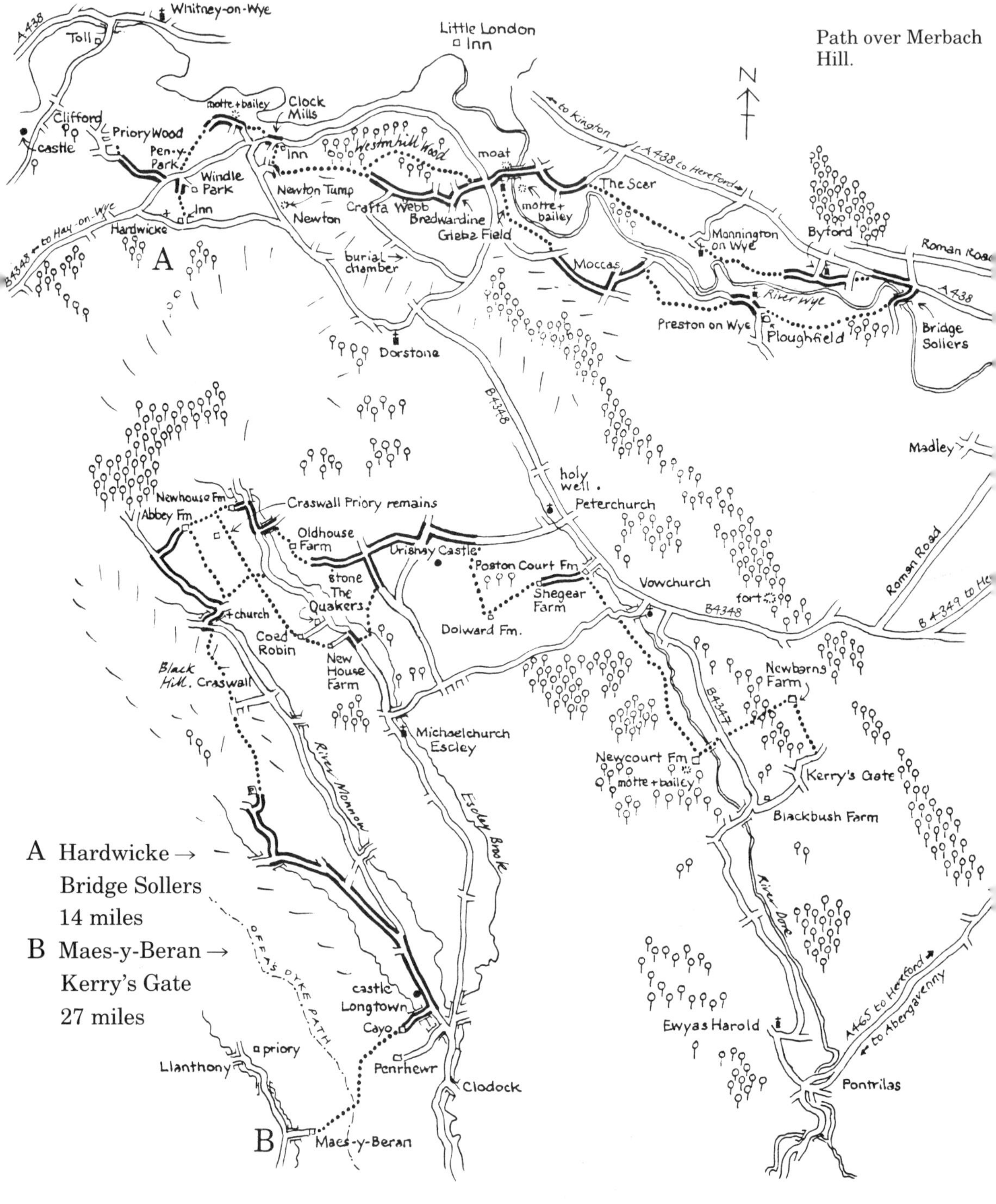

Path over Merbach Hill.

A Hardwicke → Bridge Sollers 14 miles

B Maes-y-Beran → Kerry's Gate 27 miles

River Wye by Merbach.

likely way that those drovers who planned to cross the Wye at Bridge Sollers would have gone. The other track winds its way downhill through Westonhill Wood towards the Knapp above Bredwardine. That village can also be reached by the lower path along the contour of the hill above Weston farms.

Once there were half a dozen possible fording places to choose from for those who wanted to cross the Wye near Bredwardine. The most likely one seems to have been from Glebe Field, below the vicarage where the diarist Francis Kilvert lived from November 1877 to 1879. When the course of the river deepened so that the fords became impassable, the drovers had to meet the cost of the toll bridge. The only way to avoid it would be to follow the south bank of the river on to Bridge Sollers, but before tracing that route, I should like to see what happened to those herds who did go over the Wye at Bredwardine.

The lanes going north from that crossing lead to the other Hereford Portway, also following the course of a Roman road and now the A438. There is an inn just to the east of Letton (148:338461) and from there a track goes to Little London (a name that may well, as we have seen, suggest that the drovers had plans to travel well to the east of Hereford) and to a network of lanes dominated by Pig Street and Duck Street above Staunton-on-Wye. Both those aptly named routes run north across open country to the east of the marshy ground of Letton Lakes. Such animals as were driven along them were heading for Weobley Marsh.

However, I think that most of the drovers who crossed the Wye at Bredwardine would want to avoid the tolls along the south-western Portway. So in order to reach Hereford by the cheapest and most direct route, they would make their way along the track that runs from the Scar (148:352445) through Monnington on Wye to Byford. This way is marked by the magnificent avenue of Scots pines, not in this instance indicating a drovers' inn, for they were planted in 1628 between the Scar and Monnington to mark the election of William Tomkins as MP for Weobley. A more famous politician — if so he can be called — is remembered at Monnington church, where a slab claims to mark the spot where Owen Glendower is buried. Many scholars, however, believe that the Welsh leader's last days were spent at Monnington Court by Vowchurch in the Golden Valley.

As the name indicates, there was once a crossing of the Wye at Byford. So this small village, whose church retains its twelfth-century doorway, may well have been long accustomed to the tramplings of herds from both sides of the river. If we want to follow the routes of the herds that crossed at Byford from the south, we must take the footpath from the lane that runs by the parkland of the fifteenth-century Moccas Court (148:363430), across the fields to Preston on Wye. Take the lane south to Ploughfield (148: 385414), from where a substantial footpath runs almost due east to Bridge Sollers.

Most of the cattle from south-west Wales were destined for the Gloucester markets. Many of those herds were driven east from Abergavenny, along what is now the B4233 past Raglan to Monmouth and so on towards the Severn as we saw in the previous chapter. Cattle movements across the territory of the Black Mountains were impeded by less formidable, but sometimes trickier river crossings; and whether the drovers were making for the markets at Hereford and Ross-on-Wye or heading towards Monmouth and Gloucester, they still had to negotiate the Olchon and Escley Brooks as well as the River Monnow.

B In order to reach a crossing of the Wye from the heart of the Black Mountains, I have chosen a route that starts from the crossing of the

Tower of Longtown Castle.

Honddu by the farm at Maes-y-Beran (161: 298264) just south of Llanthony Priory, where we ended the walk past the Grwyne Fawr reservoir in the previous chapter. From here a path climbs steeply into England over the ridgeway that is now part of the Offa's Dyke Path. The descent on the eastern side leads to a choice of three crossings of the Olchon Brook by the cylindrical keep of Longtown Castle, one of many fortifications along the Welsh marches. This castle was built in 1186 by the Norman de Lacys in one corner of a large, square enclosure, which is thought to have been originally a Roman garrison.

East of Longtown, there are two more rivers to cross and three more ridges to climb before the droves could reach Herefordshire's Golden Valley and the way to the Roman road that once led to the old crossing of the Wye by Canon Bridge.

There are many farm-track crossings over the Monnow leading directly to the Escley brook and the way to the east; but for the sake of seeing more of these remote and shapely hills, I propose a rather roundabout route following the old roads and green lanes that thread their contours. To begin with, this means following the course of the lane up the Olchon valley past Tir Bill Farm to the parking place at the southern edge of the Black Hill (161:289329).

Do not make for the ridge here, but follow the well marked, ancient 'summer' way that runs round the contour of the hill and is marked for most of its route by a bank and hedge of hawthorn interspersed with more recent growth of ash and alder. It now serves to separate the common land of the hill from the pastures of the valley farms. This track goes on over the hill to the stone circle by the lane to Gospel Pass, and it is tempting to follow it there; but for the purpose of following the droves that lead to the Golden Valley you must turn away from the track after it goes past College Farm (161:273362) and go downhill and across a footbridge over the headwaters of the Monnow. If this is impassable, as it may be in very wet weather, you must leave the Black Hill even earlier, and take the lane that crosses the river by the Old Bull's Head, (161:277360).

Craswall is an immensely long and scattered village. St Mary's church, by the side of the lane to the east, is well worth visiting, even if you only have time to walk round the outside of it and look at the fives court by the north wall, and the stone seat on the south side facing the preaching cross. A path from the church goes north across the meadows to the overgrown ruins of Craswall's thirteenth-century priory and the Abbey Farm. This whole area is dotted with springs, but the buildings can be reached in wet weather, when the field-path can get very muddy, by taking the farm-track (161:268372) from the lane that runs along the ridge above the east bank of the Monnow. If you come here in dry weather and manage to cross that river by the footbridge, climbing the steep hill on the other side, you will come to the lane at the entrance to that farm-track.

The next obstacle to be crossed is the Escley Brook. To reach it you must climb over the ridge of Cefn Hill, either by a short, sharp climb from the Abbey Farm, or a little more gently, by taking the path from Craswall church past Court Farm. The ridgeway here can be treacherously boggy, so in wet weather it is wise to descend as soon as possible to the lane that runs beside the Escley Brook, and which crosses it to the south of Llanrosser (161: 286380). Once across the water, you can take a footpath by Oldhouse Farm (161:295376) and Blaenau (161:297373) and go east from there to the lane that runs over Urishay Common and past the ruined castle and its Norman chapel, where you will see the remains of the seventeenth-century house built on the site of the original motte.

In dry weather it is good to walk along the ridge of Cefn Hill (once known as 'the Old Road') to Coed Robin (161:295361) and then zig-zag downhill past the Quakers and so to the lane, on the other side of which (having turned left) you will find a footbridge across the water (161:299368). It leads to a woodland path which will take you to the track for Urishay Common. South of the lane that runs from Urishay to Peterchurch, a mass of tracks link the farms on the western slopes of the Golden Valley, whose name arises from a confusion between the Welsh *dwr* (water) which the Norman French seem to have understood as *d'or* (golden). If you turn south from the castle and then turn east at Dolward Farm (161:333363), you will come into the valley by Poston Court.

A Roman road, running towards Hereford, seems to have crossed the River Dore close by Blackbush Farm, and from there headed north-east by Kerry's Gate (161:393334). To reach that point without walking along the B roads, I have taken the footbridge crossing of the Dore by the motte and bailey of the old castle by Newcourt Farm (161:374337).

To reach that point from Poston Court you can follow a series of footpaths and farm-tracks that follow the course of the river to the south to the crossing by Newcourt Farm.

Once on the further bank you can simply cross over the B4347 and climb up to Newbarns Farm (161: 385352), and from that place you can follow the side of the hill south-east below a wood, to a stretch of lane covering the Roman road, north-east of Kerry's Gate. Across the B4348 the course of the Roman road is covered by another lane, which runs east of the old crossing of the Wye by Canon Bridge (161:432414) and the lane going north to the site of the Roman town of Magnis.

The drovers from the Black Mountains that were heading for the market at Ross-on-Wye were taken across that river at Wilton (162:588243) where a stone bridge, one arch of which was destroyed in the Civil War, was built in 1599. Those who were going towards Gloucester headed first for Monmouth. For both these destinations the crossing of the Olchon Brook would have been at Clodock (161:326275). Here, legend claims that some sixth-century oxen wisely baulked at going over the Monnow. They were drawing a waggon, on which lay the murdered body of Clydawg, King of Ewyas. These animals broke their yokes in their determination, and so the poor noble chief had to be buried by the banks of the river. The church that marks that spot still retains box pews from the seventeenth century, and a stone slab behind the pulpit carrying an inscription from the ninth.

From Clodock there is a lovely path going east along the southern slopes of Mynydd Merdinn. It leads to the lanes that go past the motte at Rowlestone to Ewyas Harold and Pontrilas. It is worth following them that far, if only for the sake of the wonderful twelfth-century stone carvings of birds at Rowlestone church. They are fine examples of the work of those anonymous craftsmen who have come to be known as the Herefordshire School of Sculptors.

There is a further dramatic crossing of the Monnow as it flows south-east towards Monmouth. This route off the B4347 will take you beneath Cupid's Hill north of Grosmont Castle (161:405245). The bridge at 161:412257 is reputed to be the work of John of Kent, who came from Kentchurch on the east bank of the river. He is said to have been helped by the devil, whom he employed to transport stone to make the river crossing from nearby Garway Hill. If you decide to take advantage of this crossing of the Monnow, you can make your way towards the site of the Ross-on-Wye cattle markets by following the paths running north of Kentchurch east to Garway Hill and on past the motte and bailey at Orcop.

There are many other good things to see and fine castles to visit in the country lying to the south-east of the confluence of the waters of the Black Mountains; but there are few footpaths that can be followed for any length. The same situation applies to the route between Ross-on-Wye and Gloucester; and I am still a bit unsure how the drovers had the temerity to cross the densely wooded and jealously guarded territory of the Forest of Dean. Presumably they used the route shown in Ogilby's road book of 1675. This road ran north of the present A4316 to take in English Bicknor at 162:582157 and then went south of today's main road to go through Abenhall (162: 672174).

The Forest of Dean is a story of its own and best left for another time. Now, as we are following the cattle to the English markets, I suggest that we go straight to Newnham (162:691115) on the banks of the Severn. Livestock fairs were held here on the feasts of St Barnabas (June 11th) and St Luke (October 18th) until the outbreak of the First World War. At that time a ford and ferry provided possible river crossing which is why you will still find an inn (162:697114) on the eastern bank to the west of Arlingham. There are records that crossings were made here as early as the first century AD; and that from the fourteenth the ferry was managed by the owners of Ruddle Manor, downstream from Newnham. In the nineteenth century the ferryman at the Arlingham passage reported that he had seen as many as four hundred head of cattle waiting to cross the river for the autumn fairs. He had his work cut out, for as well as ferrying cattle, his boat was large enough to carry carriage traffic. That was a difficult business, for there was no jetty on the Arlingham side, so the ferryman had to be prepared to carry passengers across the mud.

Newnham was a busy port until the Sharpness/Gloucester canal was cut in the nineteenth century. The streets that go down to the river follow the course of the ancient rope-walks, narrow stretches of land along which the hemp to be twisted was laid down. It was from this place in 1171 that Strongbow, Earl of Pembroke, set sail down the Severn Sea to conquer Ireland. In later years, strings of pack-horses, their panniers filled with Forest of Dean coal, wound their way down to the waiting ships.

Evidence that the drovers came this way has been left behind in the name of the Walleston area in Newnham, and those of Walmore and Welchbury in Westbury on Trim, upstream, all names that derive from
C the Saxon 'Welsh'. We shall follow this route towards Gloucester by taking the main road (A48) along the river bank as far as Broadoak, an unpleasant piece of walking that can only be avoided by making your way round two sides of a triangle and taking the field-path that goes under the railway bridge towards Wyncoll's (162:695134) and then turning east to rejoin the A48 near Pound Farm, which takes its name from the nearby enclosure where stray animals were impounded. From here the riverside path, mercifully, leaves the road completely and goes through the lush water meadows of Lower and Upper Dumball, where the graziers fattened animals for the Gloucester markets as soon as the hay crop was cut.

At the inn by Hartland's Hill the main road takes over again, and follows the course of the river to Minsterworth, said to be one of the best places from which to watch the famous Severn Bore, the great wave

C Newnham → Over 22 miles

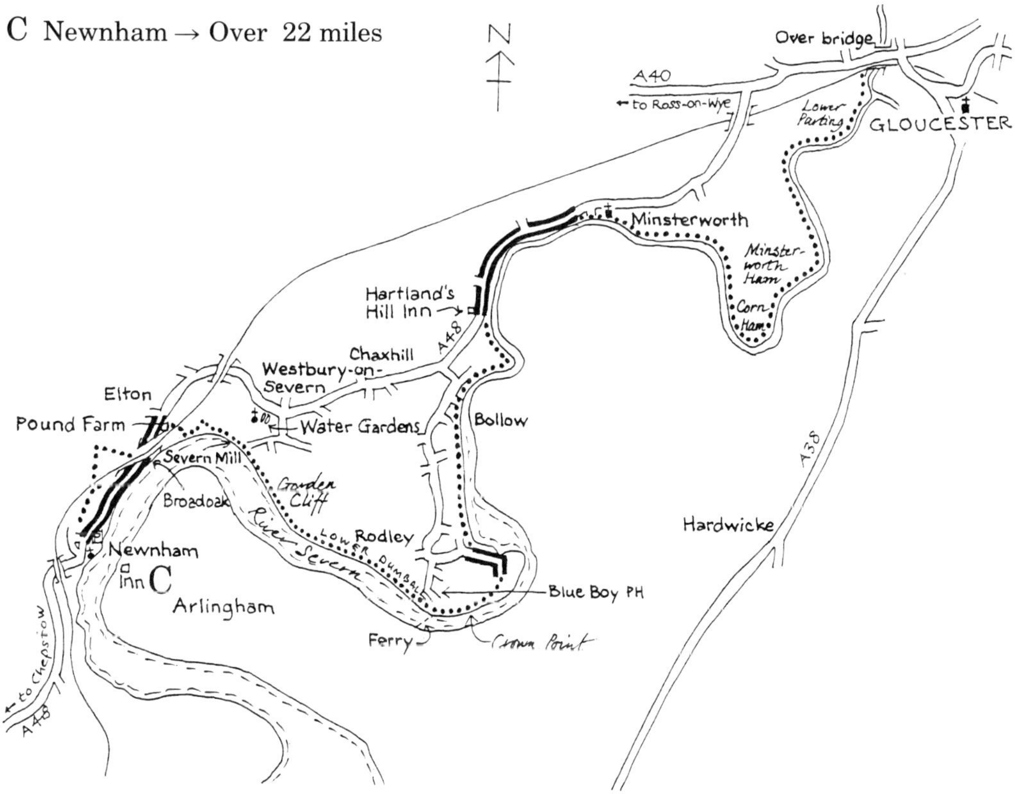

caused by exceptional high tides in the estuary, drive its way upstream. To the north, the river path winds round the four hundred acres that make up the grazing grounds of Corn Ham, and so comes to the bridge at Over (162:817196).

This single stone arch spans a crossing of some 150 feet. It was designed by Telford, and built between 1826 and 1828 to replace the narrow eight-arched bridge, badly damaged in the harsh winter of 1818. That bridge had been in place since 1540, and was the one that the drovers used. It stood a hundred yards downstream from Telford's crossing and was finally demolished in 1836.

It was not only the cattle from Newnham that came into Gloucester over the old bridge. From the thirteenth century they were also converging on this market town from Newent along a route now covered by the B4215. When the market was established at Newent in 1253, there were complaints that it would damage trade at Gloucester and Newnham, but

the case was carefully made that it would in fact enhance existing trade. There's nothing new about defending competition. H. P. R. Finberg in Volume Two of *The History of Agriculture* (1954) explains that in this case the reasons given were based on the presumption that the Welsh who sold some of their cattle at Ross-on-Wye on a Thursday would spend Friday night at Newent, because it would not be possible to reach Gloucester in one day's journey from Ross. This is based on the supposition that the drovers would not want to go by the more direct route and face the challenge of Huntley Hill (162:703188); although the presence of yet another Little London in that vicinity suggests that later drovers were more adventurous.

Those drovers who spent the Friday night at Newent would be in good time for Gloucester's Saturday market. Then, instead of pushing straight on into England, they could make a circuit and see what bargains were to be had in the Newnham market on Sunday (pre-Reformation!). Then it was back to Newent for the Tuesday market and on for a final appearance in Gloucester on the Wednesday.

From the Gloucester markets many herds were eventually driven north-east to Evesham, where the drovers spent the night before crossing the Cotswolds. Other herds followed the old Roman Ermine Street to Cirencester, thirteen miles away. The route east from here to the Thames at Lechlade is still called the Welsh Way, a name, which in one form or another, crops up many times throughout the English Midlands.

The drovers' story is unending. In the eighteenth century, ewes from Hereford and Gloucester were being introduced into Pembrokeshire. And how did they get there? Why, of course, as our old friend Charles Hassall explains, 'Our bullock drovers, returning home, bring (them) over at a cheap rate.' So, if you want to retrace your steps from east to west it would be quite authentic to do so.

Tintern Abbey by the Wye.

Further Reading

It is good news that Philip Gwyn Hughes's *Wales and the Drovers*, first published in 1943, was re-issued in 1988 by the Golden Grove Book Company of 10 Quay Street, Carmarthen. This excellently informative and most readable little book is now splendidly illustrated by archive photographs and comes with an introduction by Richard J. Moore-Colyer, who is also the author of *The Welsh Cattle Drovers*, a scholarly study published by the University of Wales Press, Cardiff, in 1976. A more general idea of the history of droving throughout the United Kingdom is given in K. J. Bonser's *The Drovers* (Macmillan, 1970) and in my own pamphlet of the same title, first published as a Shire Album in 1980; and I looked more specifically at the routes from north and mid-Wales in *The Drovers' Roads of Wales* (Whittet Books, London, 1977).

The tolls levied by the turnpike trusts were especially onerous to the farmers and drovers of South Wales, and it was in present-day Dyfed that the Rebecca Riots of the 1840s had their origin. The history of this direct action against the toll houses and toll bridges is chronicled in David Williams's *The Rebecca Riots* (University of Wales Press, Cardiff, 1954). For a more detailed account of the course of those riots on the main routes between Haverfordwest and Camarthen, turn to Pat Molloy's *And They Blessed Rebecca* (Gomer Press, 1983). Mr Molloy served in the police force as head of Dyfed and Powys CID; the close knowledge of the area which he acquired in that capacity has been put to good use in his meticulous and imaginative reconstruction of the course of the turnpike riots.

Anyone coming new to Wales will find Jan Morris's *The Matter of Wales* (Penguin Books, 1986) a marvellous introduction to this strange and fascinating country. For more detailed guides, look out for Chris Barber's walking books. They are packed with snippets of historical information and notes of little known places to visit on the way. They are published by Regional Publications (5 Springfield Road, Abergavenny,

Gwent NP7 5TD). Particularly relevant to the walks in this book are his *Exploring Gwent* (1984) and *Exploring the Brecon Beacons, Black Mountains and Waterfall Country* (1985). A more general and most valuable study of that latter area is given in Roger Thomas's *The Brecon Beacons National Park* (Webb & Bower, Exeter, 1987).

The drove routes that I have been looking at nearly all originate from the cattle fairs that were held in Pembrokeshire. For a short introduction to that peninsula turn to Brian John's *Pembrokeshire*, first published by David & Charles in 1976, and re-issued in 1984 by Greencroft Books, Cilgwyn, Newport, Dyfed SA42 0QN. For studies of the history of farming on the Pembrokeshire islands see Roscoe Howells's *The Sounds Between* (Five Arches Press, Tenby, 1968) and *Farewell to the Islands* (Gomer Press, Llandysul, 1987). This is a land of poetry, and the best companion on the walks that you will make here must be Tony Curtis's anthology, *The Poetry of Pembrokeshire*. It was published in 1989 by Seren Books (Andmar House, Tondu Road, Bridgend, mid-Glamorgan. It contains poems by such well known contemporary names as Gillian Clark, John Tripp and Leslie Norris as well as translations from the Welsh poems of Waldo Williams.

Index

References in bold refer to illustrations